Monitoring Family Planning and Reproductive Rights: A manual for empowerment

Anita Hardon, Ann Ndinda Mutua, Sandra M. Kabir and Elly Engelkes

Zed Books Ltd
LONDON & NEW YORK

This collaborative study was carried out with the financial support of the Netherlands Ministry of Foreign Affairs.

Monitoring Family Planning and Reproductive Rights: A manual for empowerment was first published by Zed Books Ltd, 7 Cynthia Street, London N1 9JF, UK, and Room 400, 175 Fifth Avenue, New York, NY 10010, USA, in 1997.

Cover designed by Lee Robinson /AdLib Designs.
Set in Monotype Baskerville and Univers by Ewan Smith.
Printed and bound in the United Kingdom by Biddles Ltd, Guildford and King's Lynn.

A catalogue record for this book is available from the British Library

Library of Congress Cataloging-in-Publication Data

Monitoring family planning and reproductive rights : a manual for empowerment / Anita Hardon ... [et al.].
p. cm.
Includes bibliographical references and index.
ISBN 1-85649-455-1 (hb). — ISBN 1-85649-456-X (pb)
1. Birth control—Government policy. 2. Population policy. 3. Human reproduction—Government policy. 4. Women's rights. 5. Women—Health and hygiene. I. Hardon, Anita.
HQ766.M53 1997
363.9'6—dc21 97-28039
CIP

Distributed exclusively in the USA by St Martin's Press, Inc., 175 Fifth Avenue, New York, NY 10010, USA

ISBN 1 85649 455 1 cased
ISBN 1 85649 456 X limp

About the Authors

Anita Hardon, MSc, PhD, received her degree in medical biology from the University of Amsterdam in 1984. She continued to do research in the field of medical anthropology on problems concerning the misuse and unregulated distribution of pharmaceuticals in developing countries. [illegible] *Ill Health, Medicines, Self-Care and the Poor* [illegible] *Drug Policy in Developing Countries* which she co-authored [illegible]. Anita Hardon currently heads the Medical Anthropology Unit at the University of Amsterdam with Sjaak van der Geest, where she also coordinates the international action-research network on Gender, Reproductive Health and Population Policies (GRHPP). Her work has been published in *Social Science and Medicine*, *Health Policy and Planning*, *Current Anthropology* and other journals in the field of health and development.

Ann Nduku Waina (B.Ed.) is a community-based health-care consultant in Nairobi. She was the principal investigator for Kenya in the Women's Health Action Foundation (WHAF)'s eight-country collaborative study which developed and tested the methodology used in this manual.

Sandra M. Kabir is the founder president and special adviser to the Bangladesh Women's Health Coalition and overseas development manager of Population Concern in London. She was the principal researcher from Bangladesh for WHAF's eight-country collaborative study on reproductive rights in practice.

Ely Engelkes is a medical doctor specialising in public health and epidemiology and has a special interest in gender [illegible]. She has worked [illegible] the Netherlands and [illegible], as coordinator of a primary health-care project in Colombia, and as [illegible] sanitation projects in Africa, the Middle East and Latin America.

[illegible] care [illegible] has been [illegible] the research manual for the assessment of quality of care in family planning programmes, and has since then been involved with the project.

Contents

Tables and boxes

Tables

Boxes

Acknowledgements

This manual is the result of a participatory process during which women's health researchers from eight countries jointly developed indicators and tools to measure quality of care and adherence to reproductive rights. The methodology was revised after having been used in eight field studies. We wish to thank our co-researchers Napaporn Havanon, Mere Nakateregga Kisekka, Micaela Parras, Maija Ritamo, Gloria Sayavedra-H. and Evelyn Schaafsma for their invaluable contributions to our joint effort.

The final draft of this manual was reviewed by a number of external reviewers: Trudie Gerrits (University of Amsterdam, Medical Anthropology Unit), Dr Malika Ladjali (World Health Organization), Amanda LeGrand (an independent researcher), Johanna Spreeuwenberg (Netherlands Ministry of Foreign Affairs), Dia Timmermans (Royal Tropical Institute), Mieke te Vaarwerk (Netherlands Centre for Mental Health), Wendy Graham (University of Aberdeen) and Barbara Kwast (Royal Tropical Institute). The following members of the Women's Health Action Foundation's Advisory Committee also gave comments: Gunilla Kleiverda, Jannemieke Hanhart, Jessika van Kammen, Floor Rikken, Barbara Mintzes and Prisca Zwanikken. The suggestions of the internal and external reviewers were detailed and precise and helped us to clarify and revise the manual into its present form.

The authors wish to thank Elizabeth Hayes for editing the manuscript, Annemarie Jurg, action research coordinator of the Women's Health Action Foundation, and Jannemieke Hanhart, who read all versions of the manuscript and spent a great deal of time editing the collaborative research study's checklists for inclusion in this manual.

The authors would also like to thank the Netherlands Ministry of Foreign Affairs which made the production of this manual possible. The assistance and encouragement of Johanna Spreeuwenberg of the Special Programme Women and Development must be acknowledged.

List of abbreviations

AIDS	acquired immunodeficiency syndrome
AVSC	Association for Voluntary Surgical Contraception
CBD	community-based distributor
CEDAW	Convention on the Elimination of All Forms of Discrimination Against Women
COPE	Client-Oriented, Provider-Efficient
DAWN	Development Alternative with Women for a New Era
DMS	Director of Medical Services
ESCAP	Economic and Social Commission for Asia and the Pacific
FAO	Food and Agriculture Organization
FGO	focus group discussion
GRHPP	Gender, Reproductive Health and Population Policies
HIV	human immunodeficiency virus
ICPD	International Conference on Population and Development
IEC	information, education and communication
IPPF	International Planned Parenthood Federation
IUD	intrauterine device
IWRAW	International Women's Rights Action Watch
LAM	lactational amenorrhoea method
NGO	non-governmental organization
PHC	primary health care
PRSO	programme review and strategy development
RTI	reproductive tract infection

SDP	service delivery point
STD	sexually transmitted disease
UNFPA	United Nations Fund for Population Activities
WHAF	Women's Health Action Foundation
WHR	Western Hemisphere Region

1. Introduction

Anita Hardon

In the wake of the 1994 United Nation's International Conference on Population and Development (ICPD), the issue of reproductive rights has received new standing as part of the development and implementation of population policies around the world. While many countries have spoken out against family planning programmes set up to achieve only demographic goals, the question lingers: Do governments actually ensure people's reproductive rights?

Many nations have endorsed international declarations which address the choice of contraceptives provided and the information and environment in which women and men should receive family planning services. However, the reality is often a far cry from such international standards. Governments must be confronted with the necessity of adopting need-oriented national policies and implementing them. Some countries are just beginning to devise new policies aimed at providing their citizens with more reproductive choice and rights. It is crucial that these countries' programmes be implemented ensuring a high level of quality.

What are some of the national family planning policies currently in place? To what extent are they demographically oriented? Do they aim at meeting reproductive *needs*? What defines quality of care and service when women and men go to a family planning centre to receive information, advice and an actual contraceptive method? To what extent are minimum standards of quality met? These are the issues that the methodology proposed in this manual addresses.

Background

In 1991, a set of guidelines for the distribution and use of fertility-regulating methods was put forward by the Women and Pharmaceuticals project of Wemos which later became the Women's Health Action Foundation (WHAF).[1] These guidelines were developed in cooperation with women's health groups in developing countries. They were envisioned as a tool to evaluate and improve the quality of contraceptive services around the world. In them, four basic criteria were selected as crucial for adequate quality of care and adherence to reproductive rights. These elements consisted of:

- the need for a free and informed choice of methods
- the provision of balanced, objective information on contraceptives and other fertility-regulating methods
- the avoidance of incentives and disincentives which may influence the choice of methods
- a health-care infrastructure which enables fertility-regulating methods to be used safely.

In 1993, WHAF decided to create an extensive series of checklists to assess more systematically if there was a gap between theory and practice regarding family planning programmes in both the North and South. This idea developed into an eight-country research project and later a book entitled *Reproductive Rights in Practice: A Feminist Report on the Quality of Care*. The study was inspired by reports from women's health advocates that, in many countries, women's reproductive rights are not respected. Using the UN Convention on the Elimination of All Forms of Discrimination Against Women (CEDAW) as a reference, the project cooperated with researchers in Bangladesh, Bolivia, Finland, Kenya, Mexico, the Netherlands, Nigeria and Thailand to examine the extent to which reproductive rights were respected and the level of care received by family planning clients.

This manual is written in the wake of the 1994 ICPD which set ambitious targets on the adoption of reproductive health programmes and improvements in quality of care. While the 1994 *Program of Action* is now setting the stage for international discussions on how family planning can be expanded to cover the whole area of reproductive health and sexuality, this manual aims to provide tools to assess if governments are actually providing men and women with access to the information, education and means which will enable them to exert the basic right to decide freely and responsibly the number and spacing of their children.

Whether or not women are able to assert their rights has much to do with gender relations, women's cultural and economic roles, and also with women's autonomy, bodily integrity and personhood.[2] The methodology proposed in this manual does not aim at elucidating the social and cultural context within which women negotiate reproductive rights, but instead focuses on the quality of care provided by family planning services as an essential prerequisite for reproductive rights to be met, while also considering what women and men view as good quality care.

Methodology

This manual presents the methods used in the eight-country quality of care appraisal. It can be used by researchers at academic institutions as well as health programmes and women's health organizations who intend to assess the standard of quality of care and the adherence to reproductive rights in family planning programmes within selected socio-cultural settings. It can help determine the extent to which family planning policies of governments (that have endorsed people's rights to access of information and advice on family planning and people's right to decide freely on the spacing of their children) are adhered to in practice at the local level of health care. To do this, the following elements of quality of care are reviewed:

- the range of methods provided and their comparative costs
- the availability and provision of balanced and objective information
- the quality of client counselling by health providers and as perceived by clients
- the use of incentives and disincentives
- the technical competence of staff and the appropriateness and constellation of the health-care infrastructure.

The research focuses on first-line services in both urban and rural areas, i.e. governmental and NGO health centres or clinics and general practitioners who provide birth control methods. An innovative and enriching aspect of the study was the inclusion of community-based distributors and commercial outlets within this group. This includes community health workers, shopkeepers, pharmacists and family planning outreach workers. The study also considers the effect that cost has on the quality and choice of services offered to clients and whether or not family planning services are embedded in broader reproductive health care.

This manual aims at sharing the methodology developed for appraisals on quality of care and adherence to reproductive rights. It will provide diverse parties involved in the area of family planning, reproductive health and reproductive rights with the tools to monitor the conduct of family planning services and to advocate for and implement improvements based on the results.

The methodology includes four checklists that aim at examining how various aspects of the guidelines compare to actual practice for use during observations and interviews with providers and clients. Focus group discussions with various groups of users and non-users of family planning services are also proposed. The checklists should be adapted to each country's specific situation (see Appendix 1).

The book is divided in the following way. Chapter 2 presents the conceptual framework of the proposed studies. Chapter 3 outlines how policies can be reviewed. Then, Chapter 4 presents the core quality of care indicators proposed for the assessment of the actual practice of family planning programmes. Chapter 5 continues with a description of the research process, the methods and sampling procedures and Chapter 6 gives suggestions for planning and implementing the studies. Chapter 7 outlines the ways in which the data should be processed and analysed, and finally, Chapter 8 discusses how the data can be used to make others aware and to improve quality of care and enhance adherence to reproductive rights in family planning programmes.

Lessons learned

This manual builds on the experience of the researchers from eight different countries who collaborated in the quality of care appraisal with WHAF. In the course of their research they reformulated research questions and refined indicators. Further improvements were made after the collected data had been analysed and reported. In the analysis phase of the data, it became clear that some indicators could not be calculated because of missing data or because insufficient observations and interviews had been done for reliable conclusions to be drawn. One major problem, for example, was the lack of data on the quality of the consultations and the adequacy of information provided to *new users*. Most of the clients in the clinics visited turned out to be existing users requesting resupply. The data on information provision to resupply clients which were collected were not relevant to the conclusions. This is due to the fact that in the cases where providers gave little information, the project researchers were not sure if this was due to the amount of information given during first consultations. Also, the data on the costs of methods turned out to be irrelevant. While researchers did collect data on the cost per IUD, strip of pills, and condom etcetera, conclusions on the way in which costs affected reproductive choice could not be made as the researchers lacked data on service-related costs. The researchers did not know, for example, how much the IUD insertions cost. They also lacked data on sterilizations as they were usually not conducted in the first-line services that were the focus of the study. The country researchers intended to compare the services of non-governmental agencies with those that were state-run. In some cases, this could not be done as an insufficient number of clinics had been surveyed to allow for meaningful comparison. The questions proposed for the policy review in Chapter 3 and the indicators proposed in Chapter 4 build on this collective experience and, therefore, put forward only those questions and indicators that are scientifically justified, relevant and have proven to be easy to answer and use.

A more fundamental limitation of the study was the lack of data on how users and non-users of services actually define quality of care. During the collaborative study, the researchers planned to carry out focus group discussions to elicit user and non-user views. Though a donor had indicated an interest in funding this qualitative part of the project, at the last moment, when the field work was already underway, WHAF was told that the funds would not be granted. In the end, some of the country teams did hold focus group discussions using their own funds. Building on their experience, in Chapter 5 ways are suggested to assess user views of quality of care. Ideally this assessment should be used to adapt the indicators proposed for assessing quality of care in the service delivery points to local realities.

Revising and refining a methodology is a continuous process. Rather than putting forward a gold standard for quality of care and adherence to reproductive rights in family planning programmes, this manual aims at initiating a dialogue with researchers and communities on what appropriate quality of care is and how one can examine if reproductive rights are upheld. The authors of this manual do not encourage researchers to adopt the proposed methods uncritically. Instead, they should be used as a reference point and adapted to specific research objectives, and to local service realities and users' views.

Notes

1. This material about the guidelines is based upon WHAF/WEMOS (1991) 'Guidelines for the Distribution and Use of Fertility Regulating Methods', in B. Mintzes et al. (eds), *A Question of Control* (Amsterdam: WHAF/WEMOS and HAI-Europe).

2. See also Corrêa, S. (1994) *Population and Reproductive Rights: Feminist Perspectives from the South* (London: Zed Books) for an excellent book on reproductive rights. It outlines how DAWN (Development Alternatives with Women for a New Era), a network of Southern women activists and researchers, views reproductive rights.

- Appropriate constellation of services: e.g. the integration of family planning with maternal and child health, postpartum services or other reproductive health services.

This framework has been used in research by the Population Council and in guidelines for quality of care developed by various US agencies involved in family planning. It is a helpful tool for researchers who want to assess quality of care, but, as Jain asserts, it does not include *standards* for quality of care.[8] The assumption is that such standards should be developed in the programme and/or country context.

The lack of standards is a limitation of Bruce's framework and the tools based upon it. In reality, such standards are rarely defined at the country level. As a result, the findings provide descriptions of

Box 2.1

The quality of the service experience: its origins and impacts

Programme effort	Elements in the unit of services received	Impacts
Policy/political support	Choice of methods	Client knowledge
Resources allocated	Information given clients	Client satisfaction
Programme management/ structure	Technical competence	Client health
	Interpersonal relations	Contraceptive use: • acceptance • continuation
	Follow-up/continuity mechanisms	
	Appropriate constellation of services	

Source: J. Bruce (1990)

Table 2.1 Criteria for safe and ethical provision of fertility-regulation technologies *vis-à-vis* the more operational elements of care put forward by Bruce

Criteria put forward by women's health advocates	Elements in Bruce framework
The need for a free and informed choice of methods.	Choice of methods: the number of methods available as well as the types of methods for various groups such as men and women who wish to space births.
The provision of balanced and objective information on contraceptives and other fertility-regulating methods.	Information given to clients: such information includes how appropriate a method is for a potential user; details on how to use the method and its possible side effects.
	Interpersonal relations: how the client perceives interaction with providers, including issues such as the degree of empathy in the provider's manner and the amount of time spent with a client.
The avoidance of incentives and disincentives.	(Not included in the framework.)
A health-care infrastructure which enables fertility-regulating methods to be used safely.	Follow-up/continuity mechanisms: ways in which clients are encouraged to continue effective contraceptive use, including means such as reminder cards and home visits.
	Appropriate constellation of services: integration of family planning with e.g. maternal and child health, postpartum services or other reproductive health services.
	Technical competence: maintaining aseptic conditions, observing protocols and having staff who are competent in performing clinical techniques.

Source: A. Hardon and E. Engelkes.

quality of care without clear judgements on how bad or good the situation actually is. The quality of care framework also does not include the use of incentives and disincentives in family planning programmes, such as the provision of food and *saris* (clothing) to women who undergo sterilization in Bangladesh,[9] which women's health advocates oppose. A third limitation is that the framework emphasizes the *process* of providing family-planning services while paying less attention to the health-care *structures* necessary for quality of care. (Although they are included in the framework as programme efforts, structural factors are not included in the six core elements mentioned earlier.) The need to consider a health-care infrastructure that enables safe use of fertility-regulating methods has been put forward by women's health advocates as an important criterion for quality of care in response to the introduction of more complex contraceptive technologies such as Norplant®. In a study on this method's use in family planning programmes, problems of unhygienic insertion and difficulties in removal were highlighted which were, apart from the technical skills of providers, related to deficiencies in health centres' water supply and their equipment.[10]

The four criteria for quality of care which were developed by women's health advocates (see Chapter 1)[11] are an attempt to define standards for quality of care including incentives and disincentives and the state of health-care structures. In Table 2.1, these four criteria are related to the six core elements of the Bruce framework.

Indicators and tools for the assessment of quality of care

Having defined the criteria for quality of care, one must next develop a list of indicators to measure the extent to which each criterion is being met. At present, there is no international consensus on the indicators that are most valuable, reliable and feasible. The most far-reaching attempt to come up with a consensus has been conducted by the Evaluation Project of the Carolina Population Center.[12] Through a series of consultations, a set of indicators for each of the six elements in the Bruce framework was developed. The indicators have been further prioritized to arrive at the following list (see Box 2.2).

In developing this list of forty-one indicators, the Evaluation Project concurred that there are three levels for measuring indicators

Box 2.2

List of priority indicators on quality of care at service delivery points (SDPs) developed by the Evaluation Project

Interpersonal relations

- Service providers are trained in interpersonal relations
- Provider establishes rapport for assessing personal situation (family circumstances, nature of sexual relationships)
- Client reports feeling:
  - a. welcomed by staff
  - b. at ease asking questions
  - c. treated with respect/politeness by providers

Choice of methods

- Number of methods approved for use at the SDP
- Number/range of methods available at the SDP
- Provider offers all appropriate methods
- Provider places no unnecessary restrictions on method choice
- Client receives her/his method of choice
- Provider refers client to an existing, accessible site for methods unavailable at SDP

Informing and counselling clients

- Provider demonstrates good counselling skills (e.g. providing information, eliciting information, answering questions)
- Provider has a checklist available on information to cover during counselling session
- Provider gives accurate and unbiased overview of all methods
- Provider gives accurate, relevant information on method accepted:
  - a. how to use
  - b. advantages and disadvantages
  - c. side effects (balanced presentation)
  - d. primary and secondary precautions
  - e. complications that require referral
  - f. resupply
  - g. other important information

- Provider asks client to repeat key information on method chosen (how to use, side effects, what to do if they occur, etc.)
- Client correctly explains method chosen:
  a. how to use
  b. possible side effects
  c. what to do if side effects occur
  d. when to return
  e. where to return
- Informational materials are available (printed, model, sample, etc.) on specific methods
- Privacy is acceptable for:
  a. counselling
  b. exam (if any)
- Consent form is available and signed by client

Technical competence

- Written guidelines on family planning practice are available at the SDP
- Job descriptions exist for each position
- Formal mechanisms exist to review/screen potential service providers
- Education/training criteria exist for service tasks
- New staff are trained regarding institution's guidelines
- Clinical providers have received training relevant to the job
- All staff receive periodic refresher/in-service training
- Basic items are present for delivering methods available at the SDP:
  a. sterilizing equipment
  b. gloves
  c. blood pressure
  d. speculums
  e. adequate lighting
  f. water
- Provider can accurately explain contraception:
  a. how to use
  b. advantages and disadvantages
  c. side effects (balanced presentation)
  d. primary and secondary precautions
  e. complications that require referral
  f. resupply

- Provider demonstrates skill at clinical procedures (according to guidelines)
- Provider demonstrates ability to recognize/identify contra-indications (consistent with guidelines)
- Provider avoids tests, examinations, and waiting periods that are not medically justified
- Provider follows infection control procedures (outlined in guidelines)
- All levels of service providers receive routine supervision

Mechanisms to ensure continuity of care

- Provider encourages client to return as needed
- Follow-up/return schedule is appropriate/reasonable
- Client can obtain resupplies easily:
  - a. supply of all methods offered at SDP is adequate
  - b. system for resupply is reliable (items always available)
- Clients past-due for follow-up are identified
- Clients past-due for follow-up are contacted
- Reasons for non-return are identified

Appropriateness and acceptability of services

- Clients and non-users perceive that:
  - a. privacy/confidentiality for counselling is acceptable
  - b. privacy/confidentiality for exam is acceptable
  - c. waiting time is acceptable
  - d. time with provider is acceptable
  - e. hours/days are convenient
  - f. staff is acceptable in terms of gender, ethnic group, age

Source: Evaluation Project (1993).

related to quality: (1) the manager, (2) the provider, and (3) the client. Since a number of indicators can be measured at two or even three levels, it was decided to identify the level at which each indicator was most important and to include the item only once on the list. In most cases this was the client level. If deficiencies are found at the client level, then one would need to return to the provider and manager levels (enabling systems) to identify the source of the problems.

This list lacks indicators on the sixth element in the Bruce framework 'Appropriate constellation of services', i.e. the integration of family planning with maternal and child health, postpartum services or other reproductive health services. Only some indicators on the appropriateness of the family planning services are included.[13]

This book's indicators were developed related to the four main criteria stated earlier. A description of the indicators can be found in Box 2.3. The aim was to develop core indicators that could be used by family planning administrators, researchers, women's health advocates and consumer activists to assess quality of care and adherence to reproductive rights from a women's health perspective. The list of indicators is shorter than that developed by the Evaluation Project. Data collection for the indicators is feasible within a low-budget project, and the indicators are easy to calculate and interpret.[14] They balance interpersonal and technical aspects of quality of care, taking into consideration women's health concerns. On the technical side, they are designed to assess if specific medical procedures are performed, allowing for judgements on quality of care to be made. The need for these specific medical procedures is specified in international guidelines on the provision of contraceptives. Only a few procedures are selected to indicate technical skills. By developing such a list of indicators, it is hoped that more actors will become involved in quality of care assessments, and that, based on their findings and recommendations for action, care will improve.

This matrix shows that many of the indicators used in the quality of care appraisal conducted in the eight participating countries are also included on the list of the Evaluation Project. This is to be expected because of the similarities in the framework used. The Evaluation Project builds on the Bruce framework, which has much in common with the four criteria which provided the basis for our eight-country study. One of the limitations that the project's participants noted in the Bruce framework was the lack of emphasis on health-care structure. However, looking in more detail at the indicators, one sees that the Evaluation Project's indicators do list 'basic items' that should be present for the delivery of methods. These basic items are similar to the items the eight-country collaborative appraisal listed for the criterion 'adequacy of facilities and materials'.

Looking at the differences between the two lists of indicators, the most apparent contrast is the lack of indicators on incentives and disincentives in the Evaluation Project, while four such indicators are included in the eight-country appraisal's list as related to criterion C:

Box 2.3

Women's health indicators on quality of care

A The need for a free and informed choice of contraceptive methods

1. Availability of contraceptive methods
2. Range of methods advised to female clients wishing to space births:
   a. range of methods advised to female clients wishing to space births
   b. range of methods never recommended by providers to clients wishing to space births
3. Restrictions:
   a. extent to which service delivery point providers apply non-medical restrictions (i.e. related to age, parity, marital status and spousal consent) in the provision of the contraceptive pill
   b. extent to which service delivery point providers apply non-medical restrictions (i.e. related to age, parity, marital status and spousal consent) to clients who wish to be sterilized
   c. extent to which service delivery point providers who apply non-medical restrictions (i.e. related to age, parity, marital status and spousal consent) to clients who wish to have an IUD
4. Quality of provider/client interactions in service delivery points
   a. quality of provider/new client consultations
   b. quality of provider/resupply client consultations
5. Extent to which new and resupply clients received the method (s)he wanted

B Informed choice of methods through the provision of appropriate information

1. Balanced provision of information during consultations with new clients who want to space births
2. Adequacy of information on the pill given to new pill-users
3. Service delivery points that have written information available for clients
4. New clients who have received written information at clinic about their method of choice

5. Satisfaction of new and resupply clients with information received

C Avoidance of incentives and disincentives that violate reproductive rights

1. Extent to which service delivery point providers receive incentives related to the number of contraceptive acceptors they recruit
2. Extent to which service delivery point providers receive sanctions if certain acceptance targets are not met
3. Extent to which service delivery point users receive incentives for accepting certain contraceptives
4. Extent to which service delivery points penalize non-users of contraceptives

D A health care infrastructure that enables safe fertility regulation

1. Adequacy of facilities and materials
2. Adequacy of providers' training
3. Adequacy of check-up during consultation with new users
4. Adequacy of consultations with new pill users
5. Screening of new IUD users for reproductive tract infections
6. Adequacy of advice when breastfeeding
7. Appropriate constellation of services

Source: A. Hardon and E. Engelkes.

'Avoidance of incentives and disincentives that violate reproductive rights'. This study's list further specifically assesses the adequacy of information provision to new users of the contraceptive pill, given that the pill is the most commonly used method worldwide. Such specific data collection allows more concrete assessments of the adequacy of the information provided. Similarly, under criterion D, our collaborative study pays more attention to the specific medical procedures that are required for new pill-users and new IUD acceptors. This allows for a more detailed assessment of the technical competence of providers than is proposed in the indicator list of the Evaluation Project. The Evaluation Project list includes more general indicators such as 'provider demonstrates skills' and 'ability to recognize contraindications'. The adequacy of advice to breastfeeding women is a separate indicator on our study's list. This indicator is not found in the Evaluation Project list. The attention to specific medical procedures and the assessment of advice to breastfeeding women reflect the emphasis in our approach on the safe use of fertility-regulation methods (criterion D). Finally, throughout our indicators, attention is paid to the need to counsel clients on the necessity of double protection. Clients should be told that the advantage of condoms is that they protect against STDs and HIV/AIDS and that a disadvantage of IUDs and the contraceptive pill is that they do not do so (indicator B1). The treatment, diagnosis and prevention of STDs are seen to be integral parts of family planning services, and activities in this area of reproductive health are assessed (indicator D7).

More systematic discussion of the criteria, indicators and items for each criterion are given in Chapter 4. The comparison set out in Table 2.1 and Boxes 2.2 and 2.3 aims to highlight similarities and differences between the indicators we propose and those developed elsewhere.

Tools Apart from the development of indicators, the increased attention paid to quality of care has led to the development of a spate of research instruments. Every international agency involved in family planning seems to have developed its own.[15] Reviewing these tools, few are found to be comprehensive. That is, few address all of the elements of quality of care found in the Bruce framework or all of the criteria for quality of care that this study has taken as a point of departure.[16] The most comprehensive tool seems to be the 'Situation Analysis Study' approach[17] developed by the Population Council. This approach looks at performance and the quality of services as provided and perceived by clients in service delivery points (SDPs). When using it, one day is spent evaluating each SDP. A combination of methods is used, including observations and interviews with providers and exit interviews with new clients. It provides aggregate data on family planning performance to be used by national policy-makers.

A method to be used by service providers as a form of self-assessment is COPE (Client-Oriented, Provider-Efficient services). COPE focuses on the client–provider interaction and helps providers identify problems – such as long waiting times, inadequate physical space and a lack of privacy – that require action.[18] The COPE methodology encourages utilization of the results in the health centres where the assessment was conducted.

The Situation Analysis assessment tools, COPE and most other available assessment tools[19] do not consider the way in which *non-clients* view the quality of care in the clinics. The mere fact that people are not currently clients could be related to their ideas about the appropriateness of the services. The bias towards clients shown by studies aimed at assessing the perceived quality of care is likely to result in biased recommendations for action. This is especially true as clients may not want to tell researchers negative aspects of the clinic operations, as they depend on the staff for resupply during follow-up visits. The emphasis on clients is further likely to lead to a gender bias in the study. Clients of family planning clinics are more often women than men. Gender-sensitive improvement of quality of care would ideally also address the issue of men's under-utilization of the services. Male views on quality of care should therefore be an explicit part of the studies.

In this manual, the Situation Analysis tools of the Population Council were adapted to measure the four main criteria given above. This meant that many questions included in the Situation Analysis tools were not relevant and that questions had to be added on the issue of incentives and disincentives and the health-care infrastructure. The Situation Analysis studies have focused on government family planning services. The methodology described here aims at assessing quality of care in all family planning outlets at the local level including services of non-governmental organizations (NGOs), pharmacies and community-based distributors. In addition, focus group discussions are conducted with users and non-users of family planning. A policy review is further done to elucidate national policy objectives and standards as a point of reference in the analysis of the field data. The methods are outlined in the following chapters.

Notes

1. Jain, A. K. (ed.) (1992) *Managing Quality of Care in Population Programs*, 18 (West Hartford, CT: Kumarian Press), p. xi.

2. Hartmann, B. (1987) *Reproductive Rights and Wrongs: The Global Politics of Population Control and Contraceptive Choice* (New York: Harper and Row); and Garcia-

Moreno, C. and Claro, A. (1994) 'Challenges from the Women's Health Movement: Women's Rights Versus Population Control', in G. Sen et al. (eds), *Population Policies Reconsidered: Health, Empowerment and Rights*, Harvard Series on Population and International Health (Boston, MA: Harvard University Press).

3. Hardon, A. P. (1992) 'The Needs of Women Versus the Interests of Family Planning Personnel, Policy-makers and Researchers: Conflicting Views on Safety and Acceptability of Contraceptives', *Social Science and Medicine* 35(6): 753–66.

4. Berer, M. (1993) 'Population and Family Planning Policies: Women-Centred Perspective', *Reproductive Health Matters* 1: 4–12.

5. Donabedian, A. (1988) 'The Quality of Care: How Can It Be Assessed?', *Journal of the American Medical Association* 260(2): 1743–8.

6. Simmons, R. et al. (1986) 'Client Relations in South Asia: Programmatic and Societal Determinants', *Studies in Family Planning* 17(6): 257–68; and Simmons, R. (1991) 'Methodologies for Studying Clients' Interactions', Paper presented at the seminar on Client Relations and Quality of Care (New York: The Population Council).

7. Bruce, J. (1990) 'Fundamental Elements of the Quality of Care: A Simple Framework', *Studies in Family Planning* 21(2): 61–91.

8. Jain (ed.) (1992) *Managing Quality of Care.*

9. Hartmann, B. and Standing, H. (1985) *Food, Saris and Sterilization. Population Control in Bangladesh* (London: Bangladesh International Action Group).

10. Mintzes, B. et al. (eds) (1993) *Norplant: Under Her Skin* (Delft: Women's Health Action Foundation and Eburon).

11. WHAF/WEMOS (1991) 'Guidelines for the Distribution and Use of Fertility-Regulating Methods', in B. Mintzes et al. (eds), *A Question of Control* (Amsterdam: WHAF/WEMOS and HAI-Europe).

12. Evaluation Project (1993) *Indicators of Quality of Care in International Family Planning Programs* (Chapel Hill, SC: University of South Carolina, Carolina Population Center).

13. The Family Health International Catalog also includes a checklist to assess quality which is included in the manual *Improving Family Planning Evaluation: a Step-by-Step Guide for Managers and Evaluators* (West Hartford, CT: Kumarian Press). This list contains many elements that would not be considered first priority in the Evaluation Project approach. The catalogue gives quality of services indicators developed by Management Sciences for Health. However, this set of indicators is weak on measuring perceived quality.

14. In the current study, each research team had a limited budget (US$14,000) and had to finish the data collection within four months.

15. Katz, K. et al. (1993) *Quality of Care in Family Planning: A Catalog of Assessment and Improvement Tools* (Durham, NC: Family Health International).

16. The catalogue also lists fairly comprehensive approaches that focus on provider perceptions of the quality of care elements. The Matrix approach, developed by the Enterprise Program (Hart 1991), for example, is to be used by clinic managers for routine internal monitoring and problem-solving. It looks at five quality of care areas and assesses these across three dimensions: facilities/hardware; service delivery; and client perception.

Other tools listed in the catalogue aim to assess client satisfaction with elements of quality of care, in line with the increased interest in the consumer of family planning services. The tools are adapted from social science research methods (focus group discussions, observations and surveys), and marketing research (client intercept studies, gathering data on a sample of people who use a specific method; see Green 1988). Often combinations of methods are used to assess client satisfaction. The IPPF/WHR affiliates in eight countries, for example, used a combination of exit interviews and focus group discussions. Some of the problems identified were lack of privacy and the unfriendly attitudes of some providers towards clients (Helzner and Kopp 1991).

The US-based Centers for Disease Control have developed a patient flow analysis as a computerized system to document patient flows in the clinic setting. It especially addresses patient waiting time, sequencing of patients and staff time spent on patient care. Some studies have used 'mystery clients' to assess quality of care. Individuals or couples are trained to pose as actual clients at a family planning clinic in order to examine the user's perspective. In such an approach, the advantage is that providers cannot be on 'best behaviour' as they do not know they are being observed. A study in Nepal (Schuler et al. 1985) found that information provided is often incorrect or presented in a way which drives clients away, and that the quality of services is positively related to the socio-economic status of the client.

Finally, discontinuation studies aim to find out how quality of care is related to use and discontinuation of methods. Studies conducted by the IPPF (Helzner and Kopp 1991) and Koenig and his colleagues (1992) in Bangladesh indicated that interpersonal relationships and staff sensitivity to the client's needs are important reasons for dropping out of the services and discontinuing the use of methods.

17. Fisher, A. et al. (1992) *Guidelines and Instruments for a Family Planning Situation Analysis Study* (New York: The Population Council); Miller, R. A. et al. (1992) 'Situation Analysis Study of Kenya's Family Planning Program', in Jain (ed.) (1992) *Managing Quality of Care*; Population Council (1992) *Nigeria: The Family Planning Situational Analysis Study* (New York: Population Council, Africa Operations Research and Technical Assistance Project).

18. Rabinovitz, L. M. et al. (1993) 'Client and Service Provider Perspectives on Quality of Care: An Evaluation of COPE in Africa', Unpublished report, (Washington, DC: Association for Voluntary Surgical Contraception [AVSC]); and Lynam, P. et al. (1993) 'Using Self-Assessment to Improve the Quality of Family Planning Clinic Services', *Studies in Family Planning* 24(4): 252–60.

19. See Katz et al. (1993) *Quality of Care in Family Planning.*

References

Bruce, J. (1990) 'Fundamental Elements of the Quality of Care: A Simple Framework', *Studies in Family Planning* 21(10): 63.

Green, E. C. (1988) 'A Consumer Intercept Study of Oral Contraceptive Users in the Dominican Republic', *Studies in Family Planning* 19(2): 109–17.

Hart, C. (1991) 'Enterprise and QA', in *The Quality of Family Planning Services in Field Projects: A Workshop Report*, SEATS, Columbia University, 18–20 June.

Helzner, J. F. and Kopp, S. Z. (1991) 'Quality of Care in Family Planning: Perspectives from IPPF/Western Hemisphere Region', Draft report, 1 March.

Kaufman, J. and Mensch, B. (1992) *Report on the Meeting on Quality of Care and Clinic Based MIS* (New York: Population Council).

Koenig, M. et al. (1992) 'The Influence of Fieldworker Quality of Care upon Contraceptive Adoption in Rural Bangladesh', Paper presented at the annual meeting of the Population Association of America, Denver, 30 April–2 May.

Mensch, B. (1993) 'Quality of Care: A Neglected Dimension', in M. Koblinsky et al. (eds), *The Health of Women: A Global Perspective* (San Francisco, CA: Westview Press).

Ross, J. A. and Isaacs, S. L. (1988) 'Costs, Payments and Incentives in Family Planning Programs: A Review for Developing Countries', in *Studies in Family Planning* 19(5): 270–83.

3. Reviewing quality of care policies

Anita Hardon

The conduct of family planning services is based upon health and population policies. Assessing services' quality of care must therefore start with an evaluation of national policies in the light of globally endorsed reproductive rights. Researchers should review government policies and those of intermediary organizations involved in the provision of family planning services. Central to the policy review are questions on the objectives of the policies and programmes, the targets set and any restrictions imposed by the various agencies in the provision of family planning methods, and any gender bias. Information on the history of the family planning programme and any laws on abortion must also be reviewed. In the same way, important government documents and other relevant literature sources should be collected and examined. All of this information can be used to highlight discussions within a country regarding family planning policies and adherence to reproductive rights.

Points of reference

Assertions of informed choice in reproductive health and the government's obligations regarding this have been a part of international declarations for more than twenty-five years. After such a length of time, governments can therefore be expected to have put the principles into practice. They were already put forward in the 1968 Human Rights Conference in Tehran, when the nation-states agreed that 'Parents have a basic right to decide freely and responsibly on the number and spacing of their children and a right to education and information on this respect.'[1]

Note, however, that, at the time, it was 'parents' who had the rights, not individual men and women. Individuals were first mentioned at the 1974 Bucharest Conference on Population when the World Population Plan of Action was adopted, which states: 'All couples and individuals have the basic right to decide freely and responsibly the number and spacing of their children and to have information, education, and means to do so; the responsibility of couples and individuals in the exercise of this right takes into account the needs of their living and future children, and their responsibilities towards the community.'[2] It is important to note here that the rights of couples and individuals are to be balanced by 'responsibility' towards the community and that there is no attention yet for gender-inequalities.

The proposed research methodology has used two more recent international declarations as its main points of reference to assess the policy concerning quality of care and adherence to reproductive rights in the area of family planning. The first one is the definition of reproductive rights, as stated in the UN Convention on the Elimination of All Forms of Discrimination Against Women (CEDAW) ratified in June 1995 by 140 out of 159 UN member states.[3] Important articles from the CEDAW document for this study are the following:

> 10 (h) States Parties shall take all appropriate measures … in particular to ensure … access to specific educational information to help to ensure the health and well-being of families, including information and advice on family planning.
>
> 12 (1) States Parties shall take all appropriate measures to eliminate discrimination against women in the field of health care, in order to ensure on a basis of equality of men and women, access to health care services, including those related to family planning.
>
> 16 (1) States Parties shall take all appropriate measures to eliminate discrimination against women in all matters relating to marriage and family relations and in particular shall ensure, on a basis of equality of men and women:
>
> (e) The same rights to decide freely and responsibly on the number and the spacing of their children and to have access to the information, education and means to enable them to exercise these rights.[4]

The second point of reference is the document signed at the UN International Conference on Population and Development (ICPD) that took place in Cairo during 1994. It strongly emphasizes quality of care in family planning and reproductive rights. The ICPD marked the first time that governments placed reproductive rights and reproductive and sexual health at the heart of a plan of action to address population growth. This emphasis can largely be credited to the activism of grassroots women and non-governmental organizations that raised these issues during the three-year preparatory phase. Assessing the current policies against the ICPD document provides a strong basis for action in the countries involved in the research. Excerpts from the document's chapter on reproductive rights and reproductive health include:

> Reproductive health is a state of complete physical, mental and social well-being and not merely the absence of infirmity, in all matters relating to the reproductive system and to its functions and processes. Reproductive health therefore implies that people are able to have a satisfying and safe sex life and that they have the capability to reproduce and the freedom to decide if, when and how often to do so. Implicit in this last condition are the rights of men and women to be informed and to have access to safe, effective, affordable and acceptable methods of fertility regulation of their choice, as well as other methods of their choice for regulation of fertility which are not against the law, and the right of access to appropriate health-care services that will enable women to go safely through pregnancy and childbirth and provide couples with the best chance of having a healthy infant.[5]

The CEDAW stressed that these rights should be exerted on a basis of *equality* between men and women and the ICPD document similarly notes that full attention should be given to promotion of mutually respectful and equitable gender relations, stressing also adolescents' need for services and information.

Existing gender bias in policies can lead to inequalities in the provision of contraceptives that are not in line with the CEDAW declaration. Many countries have policies that allow men to veto the use of contraceptives by their wives and few countries have formulated policies to enhance the responsibility of men for fertility-regulation matters. In the policy reviews, attention should be given to such gender issues.

The chosen reference documents emphasize that free and informed choice should be at the centre of any policy on health or population. They specify that governments have the responsibility to make contraceptives available and for providing information that enables men and women to make their choices.

Free choice Free choice means that contraceptives should be accessible to individual men and women, and adolescents. Thus, non-medical restrictions in terms of marital status, age or spousal consent are not desirable. Free choice is especially important in the case of non-reversible methods such as sterilization. The national health or population policies should note that all forms of surgical sterilization must be voluntary after the client has been given all relevant information.

Providing abortion services is becoming more acceptable internationally in order to protect women's health when an unwanted pregnancy occurs due to failing contraception or other reasons and to decrease maternal mortality. Women's organizations have long argued that prohibition of abortion is a violation of reproductive rights as it forces a woman to continue an unwanted pregnancy against her will. They argue that free choice should include the option of abortion.

Quality of care Improving quality of care is an essential means to enhance a free and informed choice. In line with the emerging international consensus that quality of care is a crucial issue, the ICPD's *Program of Action* also put forward the following specific recommendations. Governments should:

- Ensure information and access to the widest possible range of safe and effective family planning methods appropriate to the individual's age, parity, family size preference and other factors, to enable men and women to exercise free and informed choice;
- Provide accessible, complete and accurate information about various family planning methods, including their health risks and benefits, side effects and their effectiveness in preventing the spread of HIV/AIDS and other sexually transmitted diseases;
- Ensure safe, affordable, and convenient services for the user;
- Ensure privacy and confidentiality;

- Ensure a continuous supply of high-quality contraceptives;
- Expand and improve formal and informal training in sexual and reproductive health care and family planning including training in interpersonal communications and counselling;
- Ensure adequate follow-up care, including that for side effects of contraceptive use.[6]

Emphasizing reproductive health At the 1994 ICPD the reproductive health approach was endorsed, requiring a revolution in health care. It calls for family planning and health administrators to plan jointly the implementation of the programmes and to define cost-effective packages of high-quality integrated services shaped to the specific needs of diverse clients in different settings and available to all who need them.[7]

The shift in emphasis from fertility control to reproductive health has important implications for the objectives set in population policies. Where many policies used to set targets of contraceptive prevalence and fertility rates to be achieved, the new policies can be expected to include a broader range of health and quality of care objectives and should be more oriented towards meeting the needs of people rather than persuading them to accept contraception.

Core questions to be asked

In line with the above, the following questions are proposed for the review of family planning policies:

1. Does the government have a policy on population and/or family planning? If yes, what are its objectives? Specifically:

   - Does the government policy stress demographic goals? Quote these goals and describe any explicit targets; assess if there is gender bias in these goals and targets.
   - Does the government policy include any incentives or disincentives to family planning acceptors or providers? Describe these.
   - Does it include health objectives? Quote these goals.
   - Does the government policy state fulfilling reproductive needs as an objective (in line with CEDAW and ICPD recommendations)? Quote the relevant sections.

- Does the government policy state quality of care as an explicit aim? Quote relevant sections.
- What is the legal status of abortion in the country? Describe under what conditions abortion is allowed and how the law is interpreted in practice.

2. Describe the most important non-governmental (NGO) or semi-governmental organizations involved in family planning. For each of the important NGOs describe their policies on the items listed under 1.
3. Which fertility regulation methods (including temporary methods, sterilization, menstrual regulation, abortion and natural family planning methods) are provided by the important governmental and NGO service providers present in the country? Which methods are not promoted (for example, diaphragms and the lactational amenorrhoea method/LAM).
4. Which fertility regulating methods are available in pharmacies and drugstores? Are prescriptions necessary? Do family planning agencies make contraceptives available through pharmacies? If yes, which methods?
5. For each organization involved in family planning describe the referral mechanisms. If a client wants a method that is not available in the community-based centre or service delivery point, how is (s)he referred? To where? What are the costs?
6. For each agency providing family planning (including pharmacies) describe the restrictions that they set in the provision of fertility-regulating technologies, in terms of age, number of children, marital status or spousal approval. Also examine if this is set out in government policy.
7. For each agency providing family planning (including pharmacies) describe if and how much people must pay for each of the methods provided, including mechanisms for reimbursement by insurance companies. Describe both method and service-related costs. For each agency describe the financing profile. Where does income for the conduct of family planning programmes come from? Are user fees part of the financing system? Do providers receive fixed salaries or payment related to the number of clients?
8. Do the agencies have explicit mechanisms for ensuring free and informed choice for sterilization? Are the mechanisms the same for men and women?

9. For each agency (and the government) describe if standard guidelines for the provision of family planning methods exist. Who was involved in developing these? Specifically, have women's health advocates been involved? Are they widely used? Describe them, what topics are covered (communication skills, knowledge of contraindications and method side effects, respect for clients, privacy, necessity of free and informed choice of methods, technical skills)?
10. For each agency (and the government) describe what is done in terms of training and supervision of providers. What topics are covered in the training (communication skills, knowledge of contraindications and method side effects, respect for clients, privacy, free and informed choice of methods, technical skills)?
11. For each agency (and the government) describe if they have information, education and communication (IEC) activities directed towards clients. Describe the types of IEC activities that they conduct and the coverage of these activities. How are women and men portrayed, in which gender roles? What 'ideal' is reflected in the messages for family size and lifestyle?
12. For each agency (and the government) describe if family planning services are integrated in other reproductive health-care services, and if so, how? Specify the extent to which STD prevention and cure; maternal and child care; prevention and treatment of infertility and HIV/AIDS care, screening and treatment of reproductive cancer; safe abortion services and counselling on sexuality are part of the services.
13. For each agency describe if community-based distribution of contraceptives is part of the services, and if so, how community-based distributors are selected and trained, what method they provide and what referral options are available to their clients. Also, are they instructed to respect confidentiality and privacy of clients? Are they volunteers or paid workers?

Apart from this review of the existing family planning policies and programmes, the researchers should review other documents to obtain background data on contraceptive use in the country, reasons for discontinuation and non-use, contraception sources, demographic data and data on women's health. Such data are usually available from the national population commission or national family planning agency and from the demographic and health surveys that are done regularly in most developing countries.[8]

Interviews with key informants can be used to fill in any details needed to complete the policy analysis and are often necessary to obtain unpublished documents. Based on the policy review, researchers can identify specific issues that need to be studied at the operational level of the family planning programme, i.e. the service delivery points where clients go for contraceptive services. The indicators included in the next chapter can be revised to cover the issues of concern (see also Chapter 5 and Appendix 1 where concrete suggestions are made for the revision).

Notes

1. United Nations (1968) *Final Act of the International Conference on Human Rights*, A/Conf.32/41 (New York: UN).
2. United Nations (1974) *Report of the United Nations World Population Conference*, A/Conf.60/19 (New York: UN), paragraph 14(f)
3. International Planned Parenthood Federation(IPPF)/IWRAW (1995) Reproductive Rights Wall Chart (London: IPPF Distribution Unit).
4. United Nations (1979) *UN Convention on the Elimination of All Forms of Discrimination Against Women*, (CEDAW) GAOR Supplement No. 21, A/34/46, UN Doc. A/Res/34/180 (New York: UN).
5. United Nations (1994) ICPD *Program of Action* (UN International Conference on Population and Development; text dated 19 September 1994 (New York: ICPD Secretariat), see paragraph 7.2.
6. As summarized in Alcala, M. (1994) *Action for the 21st Century, Reproductive Health and Rights For All: Summary Report of Recommended Actions on Reproductive Health and Rights in the Cairo ICPD Program of Action* (New York: Family Care International). This is based on the ICPD *Program of Action*'s paragraphs 7.5a; 7.21; 7.23a–g; and 11.21.
7. Aitken, I. and Reichenbach, L. (1994) 'Reproductive and Sexual Health Services: Expanding Access and Enhancing Quality', in G. Sen et al. (eds), *Population Policies Reconsidered: Health, Empowerment and Rights*, Harvard Series on Population and International Health (Boston, MA: Harvard University Press).
8. Demographic and health surveys are conducted by Macro International in collaboration with national institutions. Reports can be ordered from: Macro International, 11785 Beltsville Drive, Suite 300, Calverton, MD 20705, US.

4. Core quality of care indicators

Anita Hardon and Elly Engelkes

To carry out the study, core indicators have been defined to measure the extent to which four basic criteria are being met by the services that provide fertility-regulation methods. All of them are easy to calculate and the data needed for their calculation are not difficult to gather. The information required to calculate these indicators can be collected by non-medical researchers.

The number of indicators has been kept very limited. This means that many interesting measures have been excluded so that the focus could be placed on those that give the most relevant and reliable information for each criterion. Researchers are, of course, free to add additional indicators to the original list. They should also feel free to adapt the indicators proposed so that they relate to the local setting's standards for quality of care (see also Chapter 5 and Appendix 1 where mechanisms for this adaptation are outlined).

The reader will find that some of the indicators can be measured using different data sets, i.e. from observations and from exit interviews. When this is the case, it is mentioned in the text.

In the study that led to the development of these indicators, the researchers were found to have calculated the indicators in many different ways, diminishing the comparability of the results. To ensure more standardized results, here the calculation process is described in detail. In some cases, an indicator involves a number of different items.

A. The need for a free and informed choice of contraceptive methods

A choice of methods refers to both the number of methods offered on a reliable basis and their intrinsic variability.[1] A reliable basis implies that the methods are rarely out of stock. Ideally, a client should be able to get the method of choice during any given visit to a service delivery point.

Defining a satisfactory choice is not easily done. Minimal requirements regarding intrinsic variability at service delivery points are:

- the services provide contraceptive options for men and women
- the services provide user-controlled methods such as pills and barrier methods
- the services provide temporary and permanent methods
- the services provide hormonal as well as non-hormonal methods
- the services provide safe contraception options for breastfeeding women
- the services provide postcoital methods including emergency contraception, menstrual regulation and abortion.

Providers should give clients advice on a range of methods. By presenting providers with a hypothetical client who wants to space her children, and asking what his/her advice would be and what (s)he would *never* advise, an assessment can be made of the choice that providers are likely to give.

Free choice is embedded in the provider–client encounter. It is essential that providers treat their clients in a friendly manner and with respect. They should also encourage them to discuss their reproductive goals and make a choice from among the presented contraceptive options. A determination of the quality of providers' interpersonal contact should be done based on observations of consultations and the information provided by users in exit interviews. Users often complain that providers are rude and uninterested in clients' needs.

Free choice also means that people can get the contraceptive option they want without services placing any restrictions on their availability on the grounds of age, marital status or spousal consent. It also means that people should receive advice on referral services if the method that suits them is not available. Referral for IUD insertion or the administration of injections can be necessary if there is a lack of equipment at the service delivery point, or, as is the case for community-based distributors, if the service providers lack the technical skills for safe administration.

A1 Availability of contraceptive methods

Purpose To measure the intrinsic variability of methods provided at service delivery points.

Method Provider interviews and observation of stock. A list must be made of all contraceptives and postcoital methods. The investigator must observe the presence of the method in the service delivery point.

Calculation Percentage. This is calculated by dividing the number of service delivery points which have the specified products actually in stock by the total number of service delivery points included in the study and multiplying by 100.

A2 Range of methods advised to female clients wishing to space births

A2a Methods advised to female clients wishing to space births

Purpose To assess which methods providers would advise to a woman who cites her reproductive goal as wanting to space her children.

Method Provider interviews. The question is posed to the provider during the provider interview in the form of a hypothetical question: 'What would you advise to a female client who wishes to space births?'

Calculation Percentage. This is calculated by dividing the number of providers mentioning a specific method by the total number of providers interviewed, and multiplying by 100.

A2b Methods never recommended by providers to clients wishing to space births

Purpose To assess which methods providers would never advise to a woman who cites her reproductive goal as wanting to space her children.

Method Provider interviews. The question is posed to the provider during the provider interview in the form of a hypothetical question: 'What would you *never* advise to a female client who wishes to space births?'

Calculation Percentage. This is calculated by dividing the number of providers mentioning that (s)he would never recommend the specific method by the total number of providers interviewed, and multiplying by 100.

A3 Restrictions

A3a Service delivery point providers who apply non-medical restrictions (i.e. related to age, parity, marital status and spousal consent) in the provision of the contraceptive pill

Purpose To measure the extent to which non-medical restrictions are applied in the provision of the contraceptive pill.

Method Provider interviews. Investigators should probe on what the exact age is above or under which provision of the pill is restricted, if the number of children is used as a limit and why, how marital status is checked and in what manner spousal consent is obtained (written or oral). Interviewers should probe on the reasons for the restrictions.

Calculation Percentage. This is calculated by dividing the number of providers which report that they apply specific restrictions (related to age, parity, marital status and/or spousal consent) by the total number of providers interviewed, and multiplying by 100. In addition, a qualitative description should be given of the reasons providers give for applying the restrictions.

A3b Service delivery point providers who apply non-medical restrictions (i.e. related to age, parity, marital status and spousal consent) to clients who wish to be sterilized

Purpose To measure the extent to which non-medical restrictions are applied to male and female clients who wish to be sterilized; and to assess if there is a gender bias in the restrictions applied.

Method Provider interviews. Investigators should probe on what the exact age is above or under which access to female and male sterilization services is restricted, and also what number of children is used as a limit, if marital status is required, and if and in what manner spousal consent (oral or written) is required. They should also describe qualitatively any age restrictions and restrictions based upon a client's number of children.

Calculation Percentage. This is calculated by dividing the number of providers which report that they apply specific restrictions (related to age, number of children, marital status and spousal consent) by the total number of providers interviewed and multiplying by 100.

A3c Service delivery point providers who apply non-medical restrictions (i.e. related to age, parity, marital status and spousal consent) to clients who wish to have an IUD

Purpose To measure the extent to which non-medical restrictions are applied to clients who wish to have an IUD.

Method Provider interviews. Investigators should probe on what the exact age is above or under which access to the IUD is restricted, and also what number of children is used as a limit, if marital status is required, and if and in what manner spousal consent is required. They should also describe qualitatively any age restrictions and/or restrictions relating to a client's number of children.[2]

Calculation Percentage. This is calculated by dividing the number of providers which report that they apply specific restrictions (related to age, parity, marital status and/or spousal consent) by the total number of providers interviewed, and multiplying by 100.

A4 Quality of provider/client interactions in service delivery points

A4a Quality of provider/new client consultations

Purpose To assess the quality of the provider/*new client* interaction.

Method Observation of consultations. The investigator should observe consultations with new clients in the selected service delivery points. Observing new clients can pose a problem as most service delivery point clients come for resupply and the interviewer may need to wait for some time to observe consultations with new clients.

Calculation The quality of provider/client interactions is described by referring to six items:

- The percentage of consultations in which a *friendly greeting* is given.
- The percentage of consultations in which the provider *enquires about reproductive plans and/or contraceptive intentions.*

- The percentage of consultations in which the provider *discusses methods other than the one accepted by the client.*
- The percentage of consultations in which the *client is encouraged to decide* her/himself which method (s)he wants.
- The percentage of consultations in which the provider asks if the *client wants to ask a question.*
- The percentage of consultations in which the provider *listens attentively* to the client.

Each of these indicators is calculated by dividing the total number of consultations with new clients in which the item is valued positively, by the total number of consultations with new clients that were observed, and multiplying by 100.

A4b Quality of provider/resupply client consultations

Purpose To assess the quality of the provider/client interaction by observing the way the provider greets the *resupply* client, if the provider inquires about the client's experiences with the used method, and if (s)he listens to the client.

Method Observation of consultations. The investigator should observe consultations with resupply clients in the selected service delivery points.

Calculation The quality of provider/client interactions is described by referring to three items:

- The percentage of consultations in which a *friendly greeting* is given.
- The percentage of consultations in which the provider *inquires about the experiences with the method* used.
- The percentage of consultations in which the provider *listens attentively* to the client.

A5 Consultations in which the new and resupply client received the method (s)he wanted

Purpose To assess if new and resupply clients can get the method they want at the clinic; and if not, why not?

Method Exit interviews with clients. The numerators in this case are the number of new clients who indicated in the exit interviews that they had a clear idea of the method they wanted to obtain at the clinic, and the number of resupply clients. For clients who did *not* receive what they wanted, a frequency distribution of the reasons why should be done (this may be due to contraindications) for both the new clients and the resupply clients.

Calculation Percentage. This is calculated by dividing the number of clients who received what they wanted by the number of clients who knew what they wanted when visiting the service delivery point, and multiplying by 100. The percentage is calculated separately for new and for resupply clients. A qualitative description should be made of referrals, if any. Where are clients referred to?

B. Informed choice of methods through the provision of appropriate information

For clients to make an informed choice about their contraceptive options they need to be informed on the relative risks and benefits of the contraceptives from which they can choose. This is especially so for new users, who have not yet received information during earlier consultations.

Information on the choice of methods available, how effective methods are in preventing pregnancy and in preventing STD/HIV transmission and the possible side effects should be given by providers to clients during the consultation. This information should be understood by the client and help the client to make an informed choice. Informed choice is enhanced if written (or other printed) information is available at the service delivery point such as leaflets with written text and/or drawings and pictures to clarify points. Even in areas with high illiteracy rates, written information is important as people can go to educated people in the community to have the text explained. Information can also take the form of posters, or a group discussion or displays of the contraceptives.

Once a method has been selected, it is important that clients receive more detailed information on how that method should be used, what to do if side effects occur and when to return to the clinic. An indicator is included that assesses the adequacy of information provision to new *pill*-users. The pill was selected for this indicator because it is the most commonly used birth-spacing method worldwide. Similar indicators can be made for other contraceptives.

B1 Balanced provision of information during consultations with new clients who want to space births

Purpose To assess to what extent providers give new clients who want to space births balanced information about a range of methods.

Method Observation of consultations. This indicator is calculated for the methods that are most commonly provided, i.e. the IUD, the contraceptive pill, injectables and condoms.

Calculation Percentage. This is calculated by dividing the number of

Box 4.1

List of items to assess the provision of balanced information on a range of methods

Is information provided on the following?

- how to use the contraceptive pill
- efficacy of the contraceptive pill in preventing pregnancy
- possible side effects of the contraceptive pill
- that the contraceptive pill does not protect against STDs and HIV/AIDS
- that the contraceptive pill can cause changes in menstrual patterns

- efficacy of the IUD in preventing pregnancy
- how the IUD is inserted
- possible side effects of the IUD
- possible risks of IUDs related to STDs
- that the IUD can cause bleeding to be more heavy during menstruation

- efficacy of injectables in preventing pregnancy
- how injectables are administered
- possible side effects of injectables
- that injectables can cause changes in menstrual patterns

- details on how condoms should be used when having sex
- efficacy of condoms in preventing pregnancy
- how condoms prevent the transmission of STDs
- in addition, check if samples are shown of contraceptive methods

Source: A. Hardon and E. Engelkes.

clients who receive information on each of the eighteen items listed in Box 4.1 by the total number of new clients, and multiplying by 100. Thus this indicator has eighteen items. Qualitative descriptions should be given on *what* is discussed and how.

B2 Adequacy of information on the pill given to new pill-users

Purpose To assess to what extent providers give new pill-users adequate information on the selected method.

Method Observation of consultations. The indicator can be calculated based on observational data and/or based on the exit interviews with clients.

Calculation Percentage. This is calculated by dividing the number of clients who receive information on each of the items listed in Box 4.2 by the total number of new pill-users, and multiplying by 100.

Box 4.2

Items to be discussed with new pill-users

- explain how pill works
- explain how to use the pill
- explain what to do if a pill is forgotten
- describe side effects that can occur
- specifically explain possible changes in menstruation
- specifically explain risks related to smoking
- explain what to do if side effects occur
- explain that the pill does not protect against HIV/STD transmission, specifying the need to use condoms as well if client is at risk
- tell client when and where to get resupply of pills
- provider shows sample of pills

B3 Service delivery points that have written information available for clients

Purpose To assess the extent to which service delivery points have written information available for clients.

Method Interviews with providers and/or observations. Researchers should ask the providers if information material is available and request to see it.

Calculation Percentage. This is calculated by dividing the number of service delivery points which have written information material available to give to clients by the total number of service delivery points visited, and multiplying by 100.

B4 New clients who have received written information at clinic about their method of choice

Purpose To assess the extent to which new clients receive written information on family planning methods at the clinic.

Method Exit interviews with clients. Researchers should ask new clients in the exit interview if they have received any material, and, if so, if they can see it. They should probe if the leaflet is written in a language that the client can read and understand, and add this as qualitative information.

Calculation Percentage. This is calculated by dividing the number of new clients who have received information on the method they accepted by the total number of new clients interviewed, and multiplying by 100. A qualitative assessment is given of the extent to which the information is understood.

B5 Satisfaction of new and resupply clients with information received

Purpose To assess if new and resupply clients felt they were listened to and received information during the consultation.

Method Exit interviews with clients.

Calculation Percentage. This is calculated by dividing the number of clients who (1) felt they were listened to and (2) received the information they wanted during the consultation by the total number of clients interviewed, and multiplying by 100. The percentage is calculated separately for new and for resupply clients.

C. Avoidance of incentives and disincentives that violate reproductive rights

Family planning programmes can use a variety of incentives and disincentives to bring individual behaviour into conformity with the objectives of state population policies.[3] Sanctions and incentives are interrelated. An incentive for a particular contraceptive user often implies a sanction against a non-user. Incentives in this appraisal are defined as rewards in kind or in cash to people who have accepted a contraceptive method or to the provider who recruits the acceptor. Such rewards can be provided at the service delivery point, or indirectly by gaining access to better housing, food subsidies, free health care, employment, a higher income or other benefits which are not accessible to people who have not accepted contraception. Sanctions include penalties to people who refuse to use contraception, such as denied access to housing, loss of work permits, denial of food subsidies or placing quotas on the number of children a couple can have to qualify for free health care. Sometimes incentives are available to all contraceptive acceptors in the same way. Sometimes users of particular contraceptive methods (e.g. women undergoing sterilization) receive incentives while users of other contraceptive methods (e.g. the pill) do not. When this is the case, the incentives are used to promote certain methods more than others.

Incentives theoretically can broaden the choice of individuals and/or facilitate it. An example of an acceptable reward to users is a reward that corresponds with the expenses made to use the method, such as those related to transportation. An acceptable reward to providers is the provision of free health services to community-based distributors who in many countries receive no or very little compensation for their work.

The incentives and disincentives that receive emphasis in this study are those that diminish choice and penalize non-users of contraception and that reward service providers in relation to the number of contraceptive acceptors they recruit. The indicators can measure only those incentives and sanctions that are implemented by the service delivery points, such as limiting the access of non-users of contraceptives to health care. Other societal incentives and sanctions such as limiting access to housing should be described qualitatively in the policy review. Researchers should specify what exactly they consider to be incentives or disincentives that violate reproductive rights.

A policy which gives incentives and disincentives to providers related to the number of contraceptive acceptors they mobilize is not in line with the principles of quality of care. Instead, meeting clients' needs, not increasing the number of acceptors, should be the aim of the policy.

C1 Extent to which service delivery point providers receive incentives related to the number of contraceptive acceptors they recruit

Purpose To describe if the number of contraceptive acceptors recruited affects the remuneration of providers in cash or kind.

Method Provider interviews. The providers should be willing to talk about their income, benefits and payment mechanisms. Apart from calculating the below measure, a qualitative description should be given of the types of incentives given to providers.

Calculation Percentage. This is calculated by dividing the number of providers who indicate they receive incentives related to the number of contraceptive acceptors they recruit by the total number of providers interviewed, and multiplying by 100.

C2 Extent to which service delivery point providers receive sanctions if certain acceptance targets are not met

Purpose To describe if providers risk being sanctioned if they do not reach certain targets.

Method Provider interviews. Apart from calculating the below measure, a qualitative description should be given of the types of sanctions. Sanctions exist when providers do not get a payment or a service which they would be entitled to under normal conditions. A salary cut, for example, would be a sanction.

Calculation Percentage. This is calculated by dividing the number of providers who say that they would receive sanctions if they do not reach certain targets by the total number of providers interviewed, and multiplying by 100.

C3 Extent to which service delivery point users receive incentives for accepting certain contraceptives

Purpose To measure to what extent service delivery points provide incentives to clients accepting contraceptives.

Method Provider interviews, exit interviews and focus group discussions. Payments for actual expenses made by clients are not considered incentives. A qualitative description should be given of the type of incentives that exist.

Calculation Percentage. This is calculated by dividing the number of service delivery points where clients receive incentives by the total number of service delivery points, and multiplying by 100.

C4 Extent to which service delivery points penalize non-users of contraceptives

Purpose To measure to what extent non-users are penalized in the service delivery points when they do not accept contraceptives.

Method Provider interviews, exit interviews and focus group discussions. Sanctions can be varied.

Calculation Percentage. This is calculated by dividing the number of service delivery points that penalize non-users by the total number of service delivery points, and multiplying by 100.

D. A health-care infrastructure that enables safe fertility regulation

A health-care infrastructure that enables safe fertility regulation is not easy to define. It includes the physical infrastructure of the health facilities, adherence to certain family planning procedures (these may differ between countries), adequate training and supervision of staff and the technical competence of staff. A large number of indicators can be made to assess these aspects of quality of care. In this handbook, the authors aim to limit the number of indicators, specifically focusing on the procedures followed when new users accept the pill or the IUD and on the advice given to breastfeeding women. (Sterilizations tend to be conducted in more specialized settings, so technical competence with this method cannot be assessed in the first-line services.)

The pill is the most commonly used birth-spacing method worldwide. For safe use of the pill, providers have to check whether or not women have certain risk factors, are using medicines that diminish its efficacy, are breastfeeding (for which the combined pill is contraindicated) or are suffering from diarrhoea/vomiting (which also affect the efficacy of the pill). Adherence to these procedures is a good indicator of the provider's technical skills. High blood pressure is only an absolute contraindication if the client's diastolic pressure is higher than 100mm Hg. Women should be warned about the risk of cardio-vascular disorders. Some medicines diminish the efficacy of the pill. While using these medicines, the provider can advise clients to use condoms temporarily.

IUD-users should be screened for reproductive tract infections (RTIs) as this is a contraindication for IUD insertion. The extent to which IUD-users are screened for RTIs is an indication of the provider's technical competence. Ideally, for safe insertion of IUDs, laboratory tests should be done, especially in areas where chlamydia infection is prevalent. This is because the presence of chlamydia is often asymptomatic.

If a woman is giving only breastmilk to her child and has not yet menstruated since the birth, breastfeeding has a contraceptive effect of around 98 per cent, so other methods are not necessary until she starts giving the infant weaning foods. This is called the lactational amenorrhoea method (LAM). If these conditions are not met, the use of barrier methods, an IUD or progestin-only method can be used. Once weaning foods are given to the child, breastfeeding alone is no longer an adequate measure. Prescribing a combined contraceptive pill to a breastfeeding woman is inappropriate.

In the indicators, the authors also assess the appropriate constellation of services. At the International Conference on Population and Development held in Cairo, appropriate health services were defined as integrated reproductive health services, including health services such as maternal and child care, the diagnosis and treatment of sexually transmitted diseases and the diagnosis of infertility. Therefore, the indicators include a question on the other reproductive health services given in the service delivery points. That they are given, however, does not mean that they are integrated. Of special importance in terms of integration of family planning services into reproductive health services is the promotion of condoms for the prevention of STDs/HIV.

D1 Adequacy of facilities and materials

Purpose To assess to what extent facilities and materials are adequate for safe administration of family planning methods, and whether or not appropriate counselling is present.

Method Observation of facilities and provider interviews. Researchers should observe the centres and ask the provider about selected items using Box 4.3.

Calculation For each item, the percentage of facilities that meet the minimum requirements included in the box.

Box 4.3

Items to measure adequacy of facilities and materials

- space for changing/undressing where privacy is guaranteed
- separate room or examination area where privacy is guaranteed
- clean examination area
- water available
- blood-pressure cuff present
- vaginal speculum present
- examination table present
- equipment for sterilization/boiling of medical instruments present
- a covered bin for needles and syringes present
- sterile gloves present
- disinfectant present
- inventory of supplies
- records of clients
- written guidelines on family planning present
- written information materials for clients available
- prepackaged, sterile IUDs present
- checklist with contraindications of methods present
- addresses of referral centres available

Minimum requirements for community-based distributors

- record book present
- handbook/manual on the provision of contraceptives present
- written information for clients available
- addresses of referral centres available
- checklist with contraindications for the pill present

Source: A. Hardon and E. Engelkes.

D2 Adequacy of providers' training

Purpose To assess to what extent providers have adequate training to provide family planning services. This can be both short training courses while they are employed in the health service or training in the curriculum of their basic professional training before working in the health services.

Method Provider interviews. Providers are asked whether or not they received any on-the-job training, whether or not they participated in a training course. Researchers should also assess if the provider was trained in family planning in the curriculum of his/her original training course. Specifically, researchers should assess if providers have been trained in contraindications for contraceptive use and/or on how to counsel clients.

Calculation Percentages are calculated for the following items:

- trained on family planning in their original curriculum
- followed training courses during their career in the health services on family planning
- followed a course in the past three years while working in the health services
- received training on contraindications for contraceptive use
- received training on how to counsel clients.

The percentages are calculated by dividing, for each item, the number of providers who respond positively by the total number of providers interviewed and multiplying by 100.

D3 Adequacy of check-up during consultation with new users

Purpose To assess to what extent new users are given an adequate check-up, more specifically if:

- history is taken
- pregnancy is excluded
- client is informed about follow-up visit to clinic.

This assessment is a good indicator of the providers' technical skills.

Method Observation of consultations. Researchers should observe consultations with new users.

Calculation Percentage. This is calculated for each item separately by dividing the number of times the item was performed by the total number of new clients, and multiplying by 100.

D4 Adequacy of consultations with new pill-users

Purpose To assess the adequacy of the consultation.

Method Observation of consultations and/or exit interviews. Exit interviews with or observations of new pill-users should be done. The following items should be discussed or checked:

- smoking
- diastolic blood pressure (if above 100mm Hg, contraceptive pill is contraindicated)
- use of medicines (some medicines such as rifampicine and epilepsy drugs diminish the pill's efficacy)
- breastfeeding
- diarrhoea and/or vomiting.

Calculation Percentage. This is calculated for each item separately by dividing the number of times the item was mentioned/checked by the total number of new pill-users, and multiplying by 100.

D5 Screening of new IUD-users for reproductive tract infections

Purpose To assess to what extent new IUD-users are screened for reproductive tract infections.

Method Observation and/or exit interviews. Ideally, screening for RTIs is done by a laboratory test. However, the minimal requirement is that the provider checks for vaginal discharge and/or does a pelvic examination.

Calculation Percentage. This is calculated by dividing the number of new IUD-users in which the provider checks for RTIs by the total number of new IUD-users, and multiplying by 100. Do this for each of the following items:

- provider performs pelvic examination
- provider checks for vaginal discharge
- provider asks if user has multiple sexual partners
- provider asks if partner is likely to have multiple sexual partners
- provider advises having a laboratory test done/or has a laboratory test done.

D6 Adequacy of advice when breastfeeding

Purpose To assess if adequate advice is given to breastfeeding women.

Method Provider interviews. This indicator is measured by means of a hypothetical open question: 'What would the provider advise to a woman who has not menstruated yet and is breastfeeding a six-week-old baby?' The responses are checked and categorized into appropriate (no method for a woman providing only breastfeeding; IUD, progestin-only method, or barrier methods) and inappropriate (combined oral contraceptives or combined hormonal injectables).

Calculation Two percentages are calculated: providers who supply appropriate advice (see above); and providers who supply inappropriate advice (see above). This is calculated in each case by dividing the number of providers giving appropriate/inappropriate responses by the total number of providers interviewed, and multiplying by 100. A frequency distribution of all the responses should be given showing the variety in the answers.

D7 Appropriate constellation of services

Purpose To assess to what extent the family planning services are offered at service delivery points in conjunction with other reproductive health services.

Method Provider interviews. Providers are interviewed about the services available at the clinic.

Calculation Percentages. These are calculated by dividing the number of service delivery points where the specified services are given by the total number of service delivery points visited, and multiplying by 100. This indicates

- percentage of service delivery points where condoms are promoted to prevent STDs and HIV
- percentage where STD and HIV/AIDS information, education and/or counselling is given
- percentage where STD tests are done
- Percentage where clients can be referred for STD tests
- percentage where STDs are treated
- percentage where infertility counselling is offered
- percentage where simple diagnostic tests for infertility are available
- percentage of service delivery points where abortion services are

provided
- percentage of service delivery points where emergency contraception is provided
- percentage of service delivery points that screen for cancers of the reproductive tract
- percentage of service delivery points where counselling on sexuality is offered.

Profile of service delivery points involved in family planning services

A limited amount of background information needs to be gathered to enable the researchers to make a description of the services they have studied. The following measures are suggested.

- Frequency distribution of types of service delivery points (specify if the service delivery point is a government health centre; a non-governmental one; a hospital outpatient clinic; a private for-profit clinic, and so on).
- A qualitative description of referral mechanisms in various types of family planning services.
- Average population served (in terms of reproductive-age women), by type of service delivery point.
- Average number of days per week and hours per day at which family planning services are available, by type of service delivery point.
- Percentage of service delivery points with a doctor providing family planning services, by type of service delivery point.
- Percentage of service delivery points with at least one female doctor providing family planning services, by type of service delivery point.
- Average number of paramedics providing family planning services (nurses, midwives, and so on), by type of service delivery point.
- Percentage of service delivery points with at least one female nurse/midwife providing family planning services, by type of service delivery point.
- Percentage of service delivery points with staff vacancies.
- Average distance to referred service for emergency aid.
- Sex ratio of clients visiting the services.

- Frequency distribution of types of clients visiting the services (percentages of new users, resupply clients, and age distribution, number of children, marital status).

Notes

1. Bruce, J. (1990) 'Fundamental Elements of the Quality of Care: A Simple Framework', *Studies in Family Planning* 21(2): 61–91.

2. It should be noted that a client's age and number of children are no longer advised as restrictions to obtaining an IUD. Medically, the only restriction is the existence of a reproductive tract infection and/or the inability to conduct a hygienic insertion. However, in service delivery points where reproductive tract infections cannot be diagnosed appropriately, it can be appropriate to discourage women who do not yet have children and/or who are at risk of contracting a reproductive tract infection from using the IUD. Proper diagnosis of reproductive tract infections calls for laboratory equipment as some infections such as chlamydia do not cause vaginal discharge, the symptomatic indicator of reproductive tract infections.

3. See Tomaševski, K. (1994) *Human Rights in Population Policies: A Study for SIDA* (Lund, Sweden: SIDA).

5. Methods and sampling

Anita Hardon

Various research methods can be used to assess quality of care and adherence to reproductive rights in family planning programmes.[1] In this manual, the authors propose a phased approach, with emphasis on qualitative methods in an initial exploratory research phase; and emphasis on quantitative methods in the subsequent survey of service delivery points.

In the exploratory phase, the main research methods are:

- study of documents
- key informant interviews
- focus group discussions.

In the subsequent survey of service delivery points (SDPs), the main research instruments are:

- structured interviews (including provider and exit interviews)
- observations.

This phasing is important. Based on the interviews with key informants and the study of documents, the researchers can write the policy review that is proposed in Chapter 3. Based on this policy review and on the exploratory focus group discussions, the authors propose that researchers review the list of indicators put forward in Chapter 4. Adjustments and refinements in the proposed list can be made, thus adapting the list to the health-care context in which the appraisal on quality of care will be conducted (see Appendix 1 for specific suggestions for this adjustment process).

Adjusting the indicators will make the survey of service delivery points more relevant. First, it will show if national policies are adhered to in practice. And second, it will assess elements of quality of care that users and non-users consider important.

The survey of service delivery points does not rely solely on quantitative methods. In Chapter 4 we saw that, for some indicators, the authors suggest additional qualitative descriptions. For example, on the issue of incentives and disincentives, the researchers are asked to describe the types of incentives that occur. Or, in the case of restrictions, the researcher is asked to give details on the grounds on which availability of methods is restricted.

Below, for each of the qualitative and quantitative methods, we put forward the topics that may be researched, the requirements in terms of research skills, and the advantages and disadvantages of the method.

Part 1 Exploratory phase

The study of documents Though quality of care is now receiving a great deal of attention and detailed indicators and elaborate assessment tools have been developed, it is hard to find documents containing comprehensive empirical data, except in countries where the Population Council has conducted comprehensive Situation Analysis studies.[2] However, various documents can be found that focus on specific elements of quality of care. For example, a series of the United Nations Economic and Social Commission for Asia and the Pacific (ESCAP) deals with 'knowledge and attitudes of grassroots family planning workers about contraceptive methods'. The United Nations Fund for Population Activities (UNFPA) has published a number of programme review and strategy development (PRSD) reports that include a few observations on quality of care. There are also articles and reports on elements of quality of care, such as the costs of family planning services and the training of family planning workers. There are also self-assessments done by clinic staff using the Client-Oriented, Provider-Efficient (COPE) methodology.[3] Despite the paucity of data, it is extremely important that a review of available data is made before planning any appraisal on quality of care.

A review of documents is further required for the policy analysis. Important reference materials include:

- population and health policy statements
- family planning and reproductive health policy statements and programme documents
- standards and guidelines for the conduct of family planning services and reproductive health services
- reports of agencies involved in the implementation of family planning and health care (baseline surveys, monitoring reports and evaluations)
- evaluation reports written for donors
- records of (community) family planning workers
- published studies on fertility regulation, family planning and reproductive health services
- demographic and health surveys
- information, education and communication materials (IEC).

The following topics are to be covered in the study (see also the list of questions in Chapter 3):

- objectives of population and family planning policies of governmental and non-governmental agencies
- national health and fertility statistics
- agencies involved in providing family planning services
- channels by which contraceptives are provided
- legal status of abortion
- provision of fertility-regulating methods
- use of fertility-regulating methods and reasons for non-use
- non-medical restrictions
- informed consent procedures for sterilization clients
- existence of guidelines and standards on family planning and contraception (specifically concerning the procedures to be followed with new pill-users and new IUD-users and breastfeeding clients)
- mechanisms for training health workers
- information, education and communication activities directed towards clients and the general public
- appropriate constellation of services
- mechanisms for community-based distribution of contraceptives
- indigenous fertility-regulation practices.

Requirements Of course, the method of data collection depends upon the type of documents. Policy statements should be available from the national agencies responsible for family planning. This can be a separate family planning council or population commission, or the Ministry of Health. In addition, visits to the main non-governmental providers of contraceptives as well as to the offices of international agencies and donors are needed to obtain documents. Non-published documents such as baseline studies, monitoring and evaluation reports can be hard to obtain. In fact, it may be hard to find out which documents exist. It is best to ask researchers involved in the implementation of family planning programmes what data they have collected and if one can get access to these data. This is crucial in order not to bother people in the area with questions and surveys that duplicate work already done by other agencies.

Advantages and disadvantages An advantage to using documents is that it is usually a cost-efficient way of doing research. It is very important to check what data are available before one starts doing field research. One disadvantage, however, is that one needs consent from the data's 'owner'.

Interviews with key informants An open and informal interview style with key informants allows for a wider context of family planning and quality of care to be explored. These interviews should ideally follow the study of key policy and programme documents and be used to fill in any detail needed to complete the policy analysis. Interviewers can continue to ask questions until they fully understand the situation, using the list of topics given for the study of documents. Interviews are an essential component of the policy analysis, if only to retrieve documents that one needs for the review. Very often the most important documents are kept in people's files. Without consulting those implementing policies, much detail on the policy in practice will remain unseen. The key informant interviews can also be used to ask about the reliability and validity of the data obtained from various sources.

Requirements When conducting non-structured interviews, the interviewer should be prepared with a list of topics to be discussed. However, the topic order is not defined. This will depend on the discussion's flow. The researcher acts as a moderator guiding the respondent from one topic to another. It is best to start with a topic that is not a sensitive one and is important to the respondent. In this way, an informal, friendly atmosphere can be created, facilitating a 'natural' flow of ideas and opinions.

Recording non-structured interviews can be done in various ways. The most simple one is to take short notes which are expanded upon immediately after the interview. It is usually advisable to capture the informant's words as exactly as possible. One can also use a tape recorder and transcribe the tapes after the interview. (A one-hour interview will take about three hours to transcribe.) The advantage of tape-recording is that no information is lost due to inattention or the selective perception of the interviewer.

In the analysis, the researcher cuts and pastes the original interviews into categories that are defined on the basis of the broad topics initially used and on any other central themes that emerge during the discussions. Hypotheses that emerge can be validated by interviewing people again and by cross-checking the findings with data from the study of documents. This whole process of analysis and validation requires creativity and objectivity. It should ideally be done by the person who does the interviews.

The outcome of this research method is usually hypothetical in nature. The results are hard to generalize as they are based on interviews with a limited number of people.

Advantages and disadvantages The advantages of key-informant interviews are:

- greater depth of information
- respondents determine the prominence of the topics discussed
- the researcher has greater opportunity to understand the viewpoint of the respondent
- the interviewer can discover unexpected aspects of the issue at stake
- the researcher can ask the key informant to reflect on his/her observations from the study of documents and the key informant can draw the researcher's attention to other documents that need to be reviewed.

The disadvantages of key-informant interviews are:

- trained interviewers are needed who understand the purpose of the research and can probe without being directive
- data interpretation is difficult; one has to be on guard not to select only data that fits one's explanatory framework
- reliability and repeatability of the study is limited, as much depends on the researcher's focus and skill
- they are hard to generalize.

Focus group discussions In group discussions, a researcher invites several people to participate. They may be members of the same household, neighbours, or people who share a certain characteristic (teenagers, mothers with one child, people suffering from a specific disorder, and so on). When working with such specified groups, researchers speak of 'focus' group discussions (FGDs).

Group discussions are a particularly valuable tool for studying people's varying perceptions about family planning services. They can also be used to obtain general information about the provision of contraceptives in a community. In the context of focus groups, moreover, people may be willing to express embarrassing or socially disapproved attitudes. Teenage girls, for instance, may discuss what drugs they take as abortifacients, a topic that they are not likely to discuss when interviewed at home in the presence of their mothers.

Focus group discussions are to be used in the exploratory phase of the research to assess generally where users and non-users obtain contraceptives in the research area and how they value the services at each source. The discussions can also be used to find out which elements of quality of care people consider important and to probe why some people use contraceptives and others do not. The authors of this manual propose that several different focus groups are formed:

- Adolescents
- Women with no children
- Men with no children
- Women with 1–2 children, intending to space births
- Men with 1–2 children, intending to space births
- Women/men with completed families.

The following topics for FGDs are proposed.

- What do people do to prevent pregnancy? Probe for traditional methods and probe on the advantages and disadvantages of various methods.

- Unwanted pregnancy: does it occur? Why? What do people do when unwanted pregnancy occurs? Probe on advantages and disadvantages of methods.
- Sources of fertility-regulating methods: probe on advantages and disadvantages of various sources, including any incentives and disincentives provided at the services.
- Questions on costs: discuss costs and constraints, the implications of costs.
- Questions on the constellation of services: which services are offered? Which are not? Probe on quality: how are services organized?
- Do men go to the clinics? If not, why not?
- What is important in services from the user's point of view/user's perspective?

The results of the group discussions can be used to adjust the list of indicators on quality of care that were presented in Chapter 4 to reflect people's concerns about services. This may require adding items to existing indicators: for example, if clients stress the rudeness of personnel this specific item could be added to the indicator on the quality of the provider–client interaction (indicator A4). If participants mention the lack of toilet facilities as a problem, this can be added to the indicator on adequacy of facilities (indicator D1).

Requirements The most important requirement for a successful FGD is a skilled moderator. Group discussions, while very efficient as a data-gathering tool, are not easy to conduct. The moderator does not need to have high academic qualifications, but he or she does have to have good communication skills. The moderator's role is to

- encourage all to participate in the discussion
- stimulate discussion between participants, particularly when new information is given, or a diverging perspective is put forward
- guide the group from one discussion topic to another
- not express his or her own opinion on a subject
- not to act as an expert, but to retain control over the discussion.

The choice of venue for the discussion is also important. The venue should be a neutral one; it should never be the health centre. Small details such as providing refreshments or a snack can create a friendly, relaxed atmosphere which assists discussion.

The selection of group members demands careful planning. It is generally advisable to choose 'homogenous' groups in terms of age, sex, socio-economic status, and so on. This facilitates an open discussion. In mixed groups, considerations of status and hierarchy can affect the discussion. It is generally best to keep the groups relatively small in size. Six to ten members should be the maximum.

The moderator should be present at the venue before the participants arrive. She or he can then start talking with participants as they arrive and create an informal atmosphere that encourages group discussion. The group members should receive an explanation on how the discussion will be conducted before it begins. They should understand that their views and experiences are important and that there are no right or wrong answers.

Group discussions are usually tape-recorded. The recording should be done with care. The participants should be asked for their consent on this. However, one observer/researcher should take notes as well. From the tape, it is not always clear who is talking. The observer can also record non-verbal communication.

It is important to note that group discussions can also happen spontaneously. When speaking with one community member, neighbours may pass by. The researcher can make use of such a situation to stimulate an 'informal' group discussion. Once the discussion has started, the same skills as those listed for the moderator are required. Given the spontaneous nature of the discussion, recording may be difficult. The researcher can note statements and keywords and expand on them later, if he or she is not using a tape recorder.

Advantages and disadvantages The advantages of group discussions are:

- the method is quick and cheap
- a greater pool of expertise is tapped than in individual interviews so a more diverse picture will emerge
- the way in which people interact can also be recorded
- people may be willing to discuss embarrassing or sensitive subjects.

Its disadvantages are:

- the success of a group discussion is unpredictable
- in some cases, one or more participants dominate; the views of others are not recorded and thus they are underrepresented
- the depth of information may be limited; it is hard to probe one person's ideas, as others also have to be given a chance.

Part 2 Survey of service delivery points

In the proposed appraisals, structured interviews are conducted with both providers and clients.

Structured interviews with providers The structured interviews with providers give information to calculate a number of different indicators:

- the availability of methods
- restrictions applied in the services
- the provision of information
- incentives and disincentives
- adequacy of facilities and materials
- training of providers
- appropriate constellation of services.

Structured interviews can also be used to confront the providers with hypothetical clients and to ask them what they would do in such cases. It must be noted, however, that information obtained from observations of actual cases is always more reliable than the data obtained from hypothetical questions. However, in a rapid assessment, it is generally not possible to observe sufficient specific cases. In the proposed rapid assessment, the following indicators are calculated based on confronting providers with hypothetical clients.

- range of methods advised to female clients who wish to space births.
- methods never recommended to female clients who wish to space births.
- advice given to breastfeeding clients.

Finally, structured interviews can be used to obtain information for the profile of the clinics, including:

- the population served
- days per week that services are provided
- number and sex of doctors on staff
- number and sex of paramedics on staff.

Exit interviews with clients Structured interviews are also done with clients as they leave the clinics, so-called exit interviews. Such interviews are very useful to complement the interviews with providers and the observational data. It must be stressed that they provide information on what the client remembers about the consultation, not what actually happened. Also, exit interviews cannot be used to assess why some clients do not go to the services. In this study, focus group discussions are used to obtain more general information from a user perspective.

The indicators that are measured by means of exit interviews are:

- if new and resupply clients receive the method wanted
- if new clients receive written information
- satisfaction of new and resupply clients with information received
- adequacy of screening of new pill-users and IUD-users (can also be observed)
- background data on clients (age, sex, number of children and marital status)
- non-medical restrictions.

Requirements The provider and exit-interview questionnaires presented in Appendix 2 to measure the above list of indicators cannot be used without modifications and pre-testing. Researchers are advised to do the following.

- Reflect on the objectives of the appraisal of quality of care and review the list of indicators and items to be measured. Are they applicable? Different standards of quality of care in the local health-care setting may mean that the indicators need to be adjusted. Revise the list of indicators before adjusting the questionnaires.
- Plan the way in which the results are to be presented. It is best to design the tables wanted as output of the study before designing the questionnaires.

- Use exploratory qualitative research to find out how people talk about the topics in the local language.
- Remember that the best questionnaires are short. Leave out any questions that are not needed to measure the indicators. The questionnaires included in Appendix 2 have been shortened so as to include only the questions needed to calculate the indicators. Thus, they are relatively short.
- Translate the questionnaires into the local language and translate them back to English to check that the content has not changed during the translation process.
- Write guidelines for the interviewers, train them and pre-test the questionnaires in an area where the actual research will *not* be conducted.

If the data are to be processed by computer, then data-processing personnel should be asked for advice on the best way to design the questionnaires and code the responses. The extent to which responses can be coded depends on the questions. If so-called open questions are used, then the researchers will have to code the responses after conducting the interviews. In the case of closed questions (those containing a pre-defined list of possible answers), then each answer can be assigned a code on the interview form. This makes data processing easier. It is essential that the data forms are easy for the interviewers to use.

In the small-scale surveys proposed here, no computer analysis is needed. The questionnaires are quite short and the number of respondents is limited. The researcher can add up the results by hand. The statistics used are descriptive, involving simple frequency tables and percentages. No cross-tabulations or other statistical tests need to be done.

Advantages and disadvantages The main advantages of structured interviews are:

- data can be easily quantified and compared with the results of other studies (measuring the same indicators, using similar questionnaires)
- a lot of data can be collected in a short time.

The main disadvantages are:

- the interviewer controls the discussion and therefore may influence the responses
- no data on other aspects of the problem (not contained in a question) are collected
- the responses' validity may be low as the interview is held in an 'unnatural' manner.

Observation Direct observation produces more reliable information than interviews. In the proposed appraisals, observations are used to observe the client–provider interactions and to assess how well equipped the service delivery points are. More specifically, observations are used to measure the following indicators:

- availability of key contraceptive methods.
- quality of the provider–resupply consultations
- provision of balanced information to new clients
- provision of adequate information to new pill-users
- adequacy of health facilities and materials
- adequacy of check-up during consultation with new users
- adequacy of screening for new pill-users and new IUD-users

Observational research can be difficult to carry out because family planning personnel may not want to have an onlooker present. They may feel that it will disrupt their work. Also, if they have a researcher present, they may perform in a more 'correct' way than they would normally. Family planning workers may feel that their professional competence is being tested. In fact, in the eight-country rapid appraisal study originally conducted, physicians in the Netherlands were not willing to allow observations in their practices.

This problem can be solved by observations that go unnoticed. A researcher or an assistant can pose as a client. The advantage is obvious; it gives an unbiased picture of normal procedures. Posing as a patient, however, limits the numbers and reduces the amount of information that one can gather. One can observe only one's own consultation. In addition, one cannot pose too many questions without revealing the 'client's' true identity. While using a 'mystery client' is an attractive research method, one can question if it is ethical to pose as a client when one is not. Aware of its limitations, only noticeable observation is used as a research tool in the proposed methodology.

Requirements As is the case with interviewing, it is advisable to prepare a checklist and guidelines for the researchers. The way one introduces her/himself to those involved in the research can influence their behaviour to a large extent. If the researcher stresses that she is evaluating the skills of the providers, they will feel more threatened by the study than if a different approach is taken. The proposed checklists included in Appendix 2 contain such guidelines, but these may need to be adapted to local conditions.

It is important to record observations systematically. A checklist is helpful in doing this. However, the researcher has to be alert for the unexpected and be able to describe things in more detail, as well as noting any additional observations.

The observations proposed in this rapid appraisal are structured. However, it is important that the findings from observations are validated and complemented in informal discussions with people. For example, if a speculum is not observed, the researcher should ask if it is stored somewhere. In the same way, if blood pressure is not measured during a consultation, this may be because the paramedic at the front desk is assigned this task. As an outsider, the interviewer can easily misinterpret observations.

Advantages and disadvantages The advantages of observational techniques are:

- it can provide more reliable information than oral communication, especially when done unobtrusively
- provider–client interactions can be observed in the clinic context.

Disadvantages are:

- the method is time-consuming
- it is difficult to do, as people may be suspicious of an onlooker
- the findings need to be validated through interviews
- bias due to presence of observer.

Part 3 Sampling procedures

Sampling in the exploratory phase For the interviews with key informants, there is no need to design a sampling procedure. One should make a list of key individuals and select within the given time frame the most important people for the purpose of the study.

The focus group discussions should ideally be done in the areas where the survey of service delivery points is to be conducted. We propose that a series of seven focus group discussions be held as specified earlier. One community can be selected for the focus group discussions. However, it is better to conduct the same series of focus group discussions in another community as well, resulting in a total of fourteen focus group discussions. Contrasting communities can be selected in terms of urban/rural differentials or ethnicity.

Survey of service delivery points Researchers studying quality of care will need to select health facilities for inclusion in the study. As the proposed appraisal is low-budget, such a study cannot be nationwide in scope. Therefore, a selection of research areas will need to be made, within which health facilities are sampled, following a multistage sampling procedure.

The research areas selected for inclusion in the study can be selected deliberately. There can be various reasons to select an area. A pragmatic reason may be that, within a certain area, a family planning programme operates that is interested in evaluating its services. Another reason may be that contraceptive prevalence in a certain region is so low that the government has decided to prioritize service delivery in that area, or has set stringent targets to increase its contraceptive prevalence rates. A final, pragmatic reason can be that the researcher has a good rapport with local health providers and policy-makers and this facilitates the field work.

In the study conducted for the eight-country collaborative appraisal coordinated by WHAF, most of the researchers decided to select more than one research area to allow a comparison of quality of care. For example, in Mexico, two states with high contraceptive prevalence rates were selected along with two states with low coverage. In Kenya, urban areas were compared with rural ones.

Within each selected research area, service delivery points will need to be selected for inclusion in the study. This can also be done in various ways. It is best if the sample of facilities is representative for the area. How can such a representative sample be drawn? The researchers will first need to have a list of all the service delivery points present in the area. Then, the researcher can decide to include all the facilities in the survey or to select a random sample.

An operational problem in this procedure is that the facilities differ. In the eight-country collaborative appraisal, the researchers distinguished between first-line service delivery points:

- government health centres
- non-governmental health centres
- private physicians
- community-based distributors
- commercial outlets

The researchers aimed to include all the different types of first-line service delivery points in the list from which a sample was drawn. However, the various types of service delivery points are not always comparable. Also, the relative importance of these different outlets in terms of provision of contraception differs from country to country.

Therefore, in Thailand, the researchers decided to focus on the governmental health centres as these services are the main provider of contraceptives in the country. In Kenya, governmental and non-governmental programmes are both important providers of contraceptives. Here, the researcher stratified the health centres into governmental and non-governmental ones and compared service delivery in these two strata. In addition, community-based distributors were interviewed as a separate category of providers.

Sample size The sampling procedure followed will thus depend on the local situation. In selecting the number of service delivery points for inclusion in the study, it is important to make sure that sufficient health facilities are included in each area and stratum. If the numbers are small, then the conclusions on the differences between the areas and types of service delivery are not justified. Researchers may want to consult with a statistician on the issue of sample size. However, as a minimum, it is advised that researchers include at least ten health facilities per selected type of facility, (e.g. ten governmental units and ten NGO units per research area). Therefore, if two research areas are covered and a comparison is made of governmental and non-governmental services, a minimum of forty health facilities should be surveyed.

Selecting providers In each selected health facility, only one provider should be interviewed. Ideally this should be the person in charge, provided that s/he also conducts consultations with clients.

This is suggested as the interview includes general questions about the service delivery point and hypothetical questions on client-counselling.

Stratifying observations The indicators require that a sufficient number of new and resupply clients be observed in consultations. For the purpose of analysis, it is advised that five new clients and two resupply clients consultations be observed at each facility. This means that in total, if forty health facilities are included in the study, 200 new clients should be observed and eighty resupply ones. Within the new client group, sub-categories of new pill-users and, if applicable, new IUD-users need to be made for the purpose of calculating the indicators.

One operational problem in observation studies is that actual consultations have to take place during the visit. If this does not occur, it is important for the researcher to return to the facility. The lack of clients can be related to the clinic's schedule, but may also reflect users' views on its quality. If clinics are excluded where no clients were present during the study, then bias may occur.

Performing exit interviews Exit interviews complement observations. It is proposed that five interviews should be done with new clients and five interviews with resupply clients per service delivery point. It is not necessary to interview the same clients observed during consultations. In the analysis, the data obtained from the observations are treated as a separate data set.

Notes

1. In writing this chapter, I have made use of the manual *How to Investigate Drug Use in Communities* (WHO/DAP/92.3), which I am currently revising with my co-authors, P. Brudon and A. Reeler. The methodological suggestions for field work included in the manual were extremely appropriate to the methods proposed in this rapid appraisal on quality of care.

2. See Miller, R. A. et al. (1992) 'Situation Analysis Study of Kenya's Family Planning Program', in A. K. Jain (ed.) *Managing Quality of Care in Population Programs*, (West Hartford, CT: Kumarian Press); and Population Council (1992) *Nigeria: The Family Planning Situational Analysis Study* (New York: Population Council, Africa Operations Research and Technical Assistance Project).

3. This methodology is discussed in greater detail in Chapter 2. In addition, see Lynam, P. et al. (1993) 'Using Self-Assessment to Improve the Quality of Family Planning Clinic Services', *Studies in Family Planning* 24(4): 252–60.

6. Planning and implementation of the appraisal of family planning services' quality of care

Ann Ndinda Mutua

Conducting an appraisal on the quality of care of family planning services involves many different steps and procedures. For this reason, early planning of the work involved is essential to ensure the success of the appraisal.

Good planning has several advantages, namely: it helps implementors to devise a clear work programme; it minimizes errors which may result from a lack of planning; it avoids unnecessary delays due to a lack of preparation; and it provides an opportunity to organize both human and material resources effectively.

Planning an appraisal is not a one-person job. It requires a research team as well as necessary support systems such as a well-equipped office, transportation, and typing, duplicating and communication facilities. The team should meet regularly to make sure that the planning progresses effectively. This should be the same team that is responsible for solving problems and answering questions that may arise during the appraisal.

The research team may include the following:

- principal investigator
- advisers who can be consulted as needed, including a statistician or a researcher well trained in statistical procedures to help determine the sample procedure and size and to make a plan for data processing

- field researchers
- data processors (if funds allow)
- driver and administrative officer (if possible) to assist in carrying out the project's administration.

It is important to note that the financial status of the appraisal (that is, its budget and sample size) will determine the size of the team.

The principal investigator has overall responsibility for the research project and coordinates every step of the appraisal. This person needs to be in touch with the research team throughout the project to ensure that the results are relevant, useful and available on time. The principal investigator also needs to allocate tasks.

The major tasks of the principal investigator and the research team include:

- defining objectives and research questions
- planning and organizing the study
- modifying the indicators based on exploratory data collection
- conducting interviews with key informants and studying relevant documents
- designing the questionnaires
- training interviewers
- pre-testing the methodology and changing techniques if necessary
- processing the data or supervising data processing
- presenting and discussing the results with the research team and using the data to suggest any modifications to the project plans
- budgeting the study.

The data-collection process

The data-collection process can be looked at in three main parts.

1. Obtaining permission to proceed (including ethical considerations).
2. Selecting a research team.
3. Data collection (including, ideally, pre-testing).
4. Data handling (see also Chapter 7).

1. Obtaining permission to proceed

Ethical issues Ethical considerations play an important role in obtaining permission to conduct research. It is crucial that the effects this type of appraisal research could have on individuals, groups, institutions and communities be thoroughly considered before final plans for the research are made.

Ethical issues can apply to every step of the research process. In the choice of research questions, statement of the problem and literature review, the ethical issues to be considered could include the following:

- Are the research topics acceptable to the population studied? For example, is there sufficient consideration for religious and cultural beliefs and practices?
- Have the researchers left out relevant information in the literature review or in the justification of the research proposal because it does not support their views on the problems?
- How useful will the collected information be for the people who participate as respondents in the study?

In choosing study types, data-collection techniques, and when planning data collection, questions concerning the following ethical issues should be raised:

- Could the research procedures cause any physical or emotional harm? For example by researchers failing to observe/respect certain cultural values or traditions; or by invading participants' privacy with insensitive questions.
- Have the researchers planned to obtain the informed consent of the people, providers and policy-makers who are to be interviewed and/or observed? Will the goals and procedures of the research be explained to them beforehand and will their consent be obtained?
- Can the researchers ensure confidentiality of the data to protect the respondents?
- Should names, addresses or even village names be recorded?
- Are informants observed without their knowledge (hidden cameras)? How is this information recorded?
- Are data-collection tools developed in such a way that it is difficult to distort information to reflect what the researcher wants?

Note that researchers should also be extremely aware that advantage should not be taken of minors, mentally disabled adults or other vulnerable groups.

In the analysis and dissemination of results, the researchers need to ask the following questions:

- Are the study's conclusions justified in view of the data collected?
- Has feedback been given to the community and health staff involved in the research?
- Has action been taken to ensure utilization of the research findings and recommendations?
- Has all information that will be useful to others been presented orally and published in a form that is understandable and accessible to local staff and local researchers?

Consent to conduct research must be obtained from the relevant authorities, individuals and the communities in which the project is to be conducted. This could involve organizing meetings at district level, village level or even among a group of households. Good communication must be maintained with relevant leaders throughout the study period to ensure their continued support.

Selecting respondents Acquiring permission to proceed is dependent upon the category of the respondents to be met and interviewed. For example, during the collaborative appraisal carried out by WHAF,[1] the study cut across a variety of actors involved in family planning services, namely policy-makers, service providers (both at service delivery points and at community level, community-based distributors) and family planning clients. Observations of provider/client interactions were also done. Permission to proceed has to take into consideration such a cross-section of participants. As such, it should not be seen as a one-time event but rather as a continuous process during the appraisal period. Permission should also be obtained within the ethical setting of a given area.

2. Selecting the research team

One of the major concerns at this level of appraisal implementation is the question of who should be involved in the data-collection process. To determine this, three factors need to be kept in mind. First, the project's research design should be examined to determine what *types of personnel* are likely to be required at every step of the appraisal process. Each task to be accomplished must be considered.

Box 6.1

A case study: Kenya

In Kenya, permission to proceed with the WHAF appraisal was first and foremost obtained from the Director of Medical Services (DMS) at the Ministry of Health and a letter to that effect was granted for use within the country. Negotiating permission to proceed at this level was a great advantage, especially in view of the hierarchical bureaucracy existing within the Kenyan government. Having obtained this, the researchers found it easy to gain access at district level.

The Kenya appraisal team also had to acquire permission to proceed with provider/client observations and to speak with family planning clients. It is important to point out that the political climate in any given country during an appraisal of quality of care, and especially in countries such as Kenya where 60 per cent of the services are provided by the government, can influence the appraisal positively or negatively. The level at which permission is obtained to proceed may become a hindrance if the agenda is not clear. During the appraisal in Kenya, a physicians' strike was taking place and provider/client observations were met with different reactions due to this situation. It is paramount to explain the appraisal's agenda and objectives before further permission to proceed is granted.

For example, taking the Kenyan case (see Box 6.1), data were collected at two levels: at policy level using key-informant interviews and a study of documents, and at field level using structured questionnaires. At policy level, targeting the personnel to collect data required identification of special expertise in conducting open interviews while different criteria were used for the field work (these will be explained later). Second, it should be ascertained which *staff is available* and what additional staff would be needed. Third, it is important to assess whether or not *additional training* will be required.

In the appraisals proposed, field researchers are needed, and, if funds permit, also data-processing staff (coders, tabulators and data-entry people). The number of personnel required will of course depend on the size of the appraisal and the length of time scheduled for data collection and processing. When selecting the research team, the following factors should be considered:

- personality: members of the appraisal team must be able to work well together in a flexible way, support each other and have a friendly attitude towards respondents
- level of education and type of training
- previous similar appraisal experience
- spoken and written skills with languages and dialects
- physical capacity to do the field work
- sex (if male/female composition of the interview teams is important for cultural reasons)
- gender-sensitivity.

It is important to select people who are familiar with the project area but also to avoid using staff who actually work with providers in the area. This helps to establish friendly relations with the local people and can make it easier to organize data collection. Numerous studies have shown that respondents are more willing to answer questions asked by strangers than by people they know.

Specific requirements for field researchers The results of the data collection rest primarily in the hands of the field researchers who do the interviews and observations. They are the people who will record and report on the results of the interviews, so their selection is vital for the success of the appraisal. In addition to being reliable and hard-working, field researchers should have the following characteristics:

- ability to speak the local language or dialect in addition to the country's official language
- ability to ask questions in an organized way
- experience with moderating group discussions
- ability to record answers accurately
- a friendly and receptive manner
- ability to be neutral and unbiased in asking questions, especially sensitive ones
- availability and fitness to travel and work long hours.

It is important to employ a small number of field researchers who can be closely supervised by the principal investigator, even if this means allowing a longer period for data collection. It may be necessary to train one or two extra field researchers to use as substitutes for any who become ill or are unable to work for another reason. In the meantime, they can help with editing the questionnaires, and so on.

Training for research assistants Once the research team has been appointed, it is important to allocate sufficient time and resources for the team to learn to carry out its tasks correctly, efficiently and in a standardized way. A good training programme and a clearly written training manual are essential to developing a good field staff.

The amount of training required depends on the complexity of the survey sample and the questionnaires. Interviewers and supervisors must have a thorough understanding of all the procedures they will be required to perform. The training should be highly participatory to allow observation of the trainees. Supervisors should be given additional responsibilities.

The general topics to be covered in the training include:

- the purpose and background of the appraisal
- the organization of the research team and division of responsibilities
- interview techniques
- how to conduct group discussions
- a thorough review of the questionnaires
- explanations of specific indicators of quality of care of family planning services
- administrative details
- the sampling method
- a work schedule/time frame.

The training manual ensures that all instructions are given in a standard way. It can be written in the form of an outline which the trainer follows and explains in his or her own words. Alternatively, one may prepare a manual for training and separate instructional manuals for interviewers and supervisors.

3. Data collection

Each appraisal location/site should be visited by the principal investigator before the field work begins. It is important to meet with the local government officers and local leaders in order to introduce the research team and the appraisal to them. It is also an opportunity to explain the purpose of the research and describe in very general terms how the survey will be conducted. Officials and the community should know in time that the appraisal will be taking place and that the people coming to their homes to collect information are legitimate and reliable. It is a good idea to prepare some kind of simple, written explanation of the study's purpose to give to local authorities so that they can answer any questions directed to them by the community. Their help in arranging the focus group discussions during the exploratory phase should be requested. Regular review/progress meetings should be held by the team leaders.

Field review and quality control The quality of the collected data from questionnaires can be improved in a number of ways.

- The interviewer should check to see whether or not the questionnaire is filled in completely before the interview is terminated and make sure that the recorded information makes sense. Problems should be discussed with interviewers, and if necessary the researcher should go back to complete the form.
- Researchers should make checks during data analysis to ensure that the data are complete and consistent. Insufficient quality control during the data-collection process may result in biases in the data leading to false or misleading conclusions. Most of these sources of bias have been discussed in the previous chapters.

Supervision in the field should particularly try to prevent the following biases:

- deviations from sampling procedures set out in the proposal
- variations in interviewer style and research procedures due to deficiencies in training, poor selection procedures, stress or overwork
- inconsistency among various members of the research team – including non-adherence to standard procedures
- bias in observers' assessments because they make a mistake in favour of expected results when recording observations or answers to open questions.

Pre-testing the methodology A pre-test refers to a small-scale field testing of a particular research component. It helps to identify potential problems within the proposed study so that revisions can be made if necessary. Although this entails extra effort at the beginning of a research project, the pre-test allows researchers to encounter problems on a small scale before starting a major study. Adaptations can then be made which save a good deal of time, effort and money in the long run. The following three aspects of the research methodology can be evaluated during pre-testing.

1. Respondents' reactions to the research procedures can be observed in the pre-test to determine:

- availability of the study population and how respondents' daily work schemes can best be respected
- acceptability of the methods used to establish contact with the study population
- acceptability of the questions asked
- willingness of the respondents to answer the questions and collaborate with the study.

2. The data-collection tools can be pre-tested to determine:

- whether or not the tools used allow the researchers to collect the information needed and if those tools are reliable (some of the data collected may not be relevant to the problem or not in a form suitable for analysis; this is the time to stop collecting these data and to revise the way they are collected or to consider using additional techniques)
- the time needed to administer the questionnaire, to conduct observations or group interviews
- whether there is any need to revise the format or presentation of questionnaires/interview schedules, including: the greeting given to the person who will be interviewed; the sequences of questions; the wording of questions (are they clear?); adequate space for answers; pre-coding some answers or changing open questions; the accuracy of translations; and the need for additional instructions for interviewers (guidelines for 'probing' certain open questions).

3. Sampling procedures can be checked for the following points. Are the instructions to obtain the sample used in the same way by all the staff involved? How much time is needed to locate individuals to be included in the study?

4. Staffing and activities of the research team can be checked while all are participating in administering the pilot study to determine the following.

- How successful was the training of the research team?
- What is the work output of each staff member?
- What are the group dynamics within the team?
- Has logistical support been adequately arranged?
- How reliable are the results when instruments or tests are administered by different members of the research team?
- How accurate is their interpretation?
- How well do the proposed plans for staff supervision function?

The pre-test can be used as a period of extra training for the research team in which sensitivity to the needs and wishes of the population studied is developed.

Lessons from Kenya Data collection in Kenya did not present any major constraints but a few lessons were drawn from it which are worth mentioning here. The sequencing of certain sensitive questions presented some problems and, as a result, the team resolved to ask certain questions first and then build on these to solicit answers for the rest. Also, among the clients where the level of education was low, it was difficult, for example, to determine the age of the client. As a result, calendars of events were used to determine client age.

Another drawback experienced in Kenya during data collection was accessing the clients of community-based distributors. These distributors are not facility-based and, as a result, their clients had to be sought. Hence, it was difficult to observe community-based distributor/client interactions. The interviews had to be based on the clients' last visit to the distributor instead.

4. Data handling

Before the data are collected, a clear procedure should be identified to process them.

- Check that the data gathered are complete and accurate.
- The questionnaires have to be numbered. Decide if this should be done at the time of the interview or when they are stored. The codes should clarify where the interviews were done.

- Identify the person responsible for storing the data and where they will be stored.
- Decide which data should be stored. Storage should be organized so that record forms are logically placed in a number or data sequence.
- Decide whether the data will be processed or tabulated in the field or whether they will be transported back to the main base for this exercise (see also Chapter 7).

Note

1. See this methodology handbook's companion book Hardon, A. P. et al. (eds) (1997) *Reproductive Rights in Practice: A Feminist Report on the Quality of Care* (London: Zed Books). United Nations FAO (1988) *Conducting Small Scale Nutrition Surveys: A Field Manual by FAO* and World Health Organization (1988) *Health Systems Research Training Course*, were also consulted for this chapter.

7. Data analysis and reporting

Anita Hardon

The preceding chapters have discussed in detail the objectives, indicators and tools for the proposed appraisal of quality of care and adherence to reproductive rights in family planning programmes.[1]

When analysing the data, the list of questions formulated for the policy analysis, the focus group discussions and the list of criteria and indicators for the field study form the point of reference. In the exploratory phase, with the policy analysis and in the focus group discussions with users and non-users, mainly qualitative data have been collected. For the appraisal of the service delivery points, the data are mostly quantitative.

When working with qualitative data, analysis is a matter of describing, summarizing and interpreting the information. The researcher should start analysing while collecting the data so that questions that remained unanswered (or new questions that come up) can be addressed before data collection is completed.

For the quantitative data, the analysis aims at supplying a calculation for each of the indicators listed in Chapter 4. The quantitative measures should be complemented with qualitative observations and descriptions where appropriate and called for (see Chapter 4). It is the quantitative data that will receive the most attention in this chapter.

Data analysis, whether qualitative or quantitative, involves a number of necessary steps that will be discussed separately. These are sorting data; performing quality control checks; data processing; and data analysis.

Data sorting

An appropriate system for sorting data is important for facilitating subsequent processing and analysis. In a comparative study, it is best to sort the data right after collection into the two, three or four groups that will be compared in data analysis. If the study design, for example, involves a comparison of governmental and non-governmental facilities, then the interview and observational data gathered in the study should be sorted according to these categories.

Performing quality control checks

In Chapter 6, it was stressed that data should be checked for accuracy and consistency in the field to ensure that all information has been properly collected and recorded. Before and during data processing, however, the data should be checked again for completeness and internal consistency. If a questionnaire has not been filled in entirely, the researcher will have missing data for some of the indicators. If there are many missing items in a particular questionnaire it is advisable to exclude the whole questionnaire from further analysis.

Data processing: categorizing and coding

The qualitative data collected for the policy analysis and the results of the focus group discussions will need to be analysed using the original list of questions as a basis. The data processing will involve reading through documents, interview reports and transcripts of the focus group discussions and categorizing and summarizing the data for each research question. This data processing should be done prior to the appraisal of the service delivery points as the results are used to revise the indicators and to adjust tools.

For most of the responses to questions included in the field survey checklists (see Appendix II) it is possible to devise codes prior to conducting the interviews. Codes can be numerical (for example, the cost of a method in local currency), or simply 'yes' and 'no'. When finalizing the checklists, it is best to insert a box in the right margin of the page for each question's response. These boxes should not be used by the interviewer but, rather, filled in afterwards during data processing.

For each indicator, one or more master sheets should be prepared to summarize the data collected. If the appraisal aims to compare two research areas or different types of health facilities, then a separate master sheet per indicator should be prepared for each area or type of health facility (see Table 7.1). Forms should also be made for complementary qualitative data obtained, where relevant.

Table 7.1 Example of a master sheet for indicator A1 – availability of contraceptive methods

SDP type	Combined pills		Injectables		Condoms		IUDs	
gov't nr	yes	no	yes	no	yes	no	yes	no
1	×			×	×		×	
2	×			×	×			×
3		×	×		×			×
etc.								

Source: A. Hardon.

Collected data are much easier to tally from such master sheets than from the original questionnaires. Straight counts can be performed to allow the calculation of indicators.

When filling in the master sheets, it is important to check the totals. They should correspond to the total number of study units in the sub-group for which the master sheet is used. If this is not the case, it may be due to 'missing cases' (for some units, the information is not available), or to mistakes made when filling in the master sheets.

As plans are made for data processing, the researchers must decide whether or not to process and analyse the data manually, using the data master sheets as shown or by computer. The proposed study is designed to be small and simple so a statistical package is not needed. However, if the researchers decide to enter the data into a computerized statistical package, the statistician working on the project should be consulted as soon as the questionnaires have been made and the list of indicators finalized. A number of computer programs are available for this type of analysis. They include Dbase, SPSS and EPI Info.

Data analysis

Assuming that the analysis is done manually as proposed, the data analysis calls for calculating percentages as put forward in the description of the indicators (see Chapter 4).

The percentages are calculated as follows:

$$\frac{\text{Frequency event occurs (numerator)} \times 100}{\text{Number of study units (denominator)}}$$

When calculating the percentages, it is very important to check that the right number of study units is included as the denominator. Many of the indicators describe the situation in the service delivery

Table 7.2 Percentage of service delivery points where specified contraceptive methods were available during the survey (n = 40)

Contraceptive method	Available (%)
1. Combined pill	91
2. Progestin-only pills	81
3. Norplant®	22
4. Injectables	
Depo-Provera®	91
Noristerat®	56
5. Barrier methods	
condom	91
diaphragm	6
6. Spermicides	
foaming tablets	41
jelly	9
7. IUD	
Copper T 380A	59
Lippes	9
Multiload 375	9
Multiload 250	3
8. Sterilization	
Female sterilization	34
Male sterilization	6
9. Natural family planning	31

Source: A. Hardon and E. Engelkes.

points with the total number of provider interviews (which equals the total number of service delivery points visited) as the denominator. (For example, the percentage of service delivery points where access to sterilization is restricted by marital status.)

For the observations, the denominator is the total number of consultations observed which fulfil certain criteria, i.e. the number of *new* client consultations observed; or even more specifically, the number of *new pill-users* observed.

The data resulting from the calculation of the indicators are best presented in tables, as most of the indicators involve the measurement of one or more items. In presenting the tables, it is important that the title mentions the number of study units on which the indicator is based and describes precisely what is presented in the table.

Cross-tabulations can be made to compare the indicators by study area or by type of health facility. Tables 7.1 to 7.3 are examples resulting from the WHAF study.

In Table 7.2, it can be seen that the researcher has added specific data on the types of injectables, barrier methods, sterilization procedures and IUDs present in the facility. The table presents the information for indicator A1, the range of methods provided at the service delivery points.

An example of a table describing the adequacy of check-ups for new users (indicator D3) is given in Table 7.3.

Table 7.3 Percentage of consultations with new clients in Service Delivery Points and at community-based distributors where providers perform check-ups

	Consultations in SDPs (%)	Consultations in CBDs (%)
History taken	60	37
Contraindication checklist used	44	18
Client is informed about follow-up visit	30	45
Pregnancy excluded	50	0
Total clients observed	n = 80	n = 24

Source: A. Hardon and E. Engelkes.

Here one can see that a cross-tabulation has been made, comparing the results found among eighty new clients in the service delivery points with twenty-four new clients observed at community-based distributors.

The tables for each of the core indicators and the results of the qualitative policy analysis form the basis of the appraisal report.

The proposed study is descriptive and comparative. No statistical tests need to be done to test differences between the groups as no hypotheses on quality of care have been made and the number of study units included is relatively small. The aim is simply to give a good description of the situation, using the defined indicators and criteria for quality of care. The results indicate problems occurring in quality of care and adherence to reproductive rights. These can be used to develop recommendations for action and for further analytical studies.

Writing the report

The four main criteria for quality of care listed in Chapter 4 form the basis of the report:

- The need for a free and informed choice of contraceptive methods
- Informed choice of methods through the provision of appropriate information
- Avoidance of incentives and disincentives that violate reproductive rights
- A health-care infrastructure that enables safe fertility regulation.

The tables for each of these indicators can be used to describe the situation. A comparison between the observation results and those of the exit interviews and provider interviews should be made where relevant. Qualitative data should be used to describe the situation in more detail (see the indicators in Chapter 4 where detailed suggestions are given). These data sources are complementary. For each criterion, the researcher should make some evaluating conclusions. (Is the criterion being met? How could the situation be improved?)

If the study aims to compare types of service delivery points or different research areas, then this comparison should be made for each criterion using cross-tabulations as shown in Table 7.3.

The results of the policy analysis serve as an introduction and a point of reference where applicable for discussing the field study results. They also provide a basis for recommendations for action.

Box 7.1

Proposed outline of reports of rapid appraisal on quality of care and adherence to reproductive rights

1. Introduction
2. Short review of family planning policy and programmes in the country
3. Methods used

- research areas selected, sampling procedures
- focus of the study
- tools utilized

4. Results of the field survey on quality of care
   Family planning and fertility regulation from a user and non-user perspective (results of the focus group discussions).
   Profile of the service delivery points surveyed and characteristics of the clients.

   Criterion A. The need for a free and informed choice of contraceptive methods
   Criterion B. Informed choice of methods through the provision of appropriate information
   Criterion C. Avoidance of incentives and disincentives that violate reproductive rights
   Criterion D. A health-care infrastructure that enables safe fertility regulation

5. Main conclusions

- Give an overview of quality of care by criterion.
- Contrast policy and practice.
- Contrast what providers say they do and what was observed, and what clients said in exit interviews, and what non-users said in focus group discussions.

Source: A. Hardon.

The results of the focus group discussions can be used to outline the services and fertility-regulating methods available from a client's perspective.

Finally, when writing the report, it is important to compare the results with those of other studies already done on (elements of) quality of care in the country. The researchers should see if their results confirm those of other studies or not.

Box 7.1 provides an outline for the appraisal project report. More summarized versions can be made for the providers and people in the research area who participated in the study.

Note

1. This chapter is based on Module 24 of the Hardon, A. P. et al. (eds) (1994) *Applied Health Research Manual* (Amsterdam: Spinhuis). This manual was prepared for a course on Anthropology of Health and Health Care.

8. How to use the appraisal report

Sandra M. Kabir

The eight-country appraisals which formed the basis of this manual[1] were all undertaken in a collaborative way. From the start, efforts were made to include as many interested parties as possible. In several countries, various approaches were taken to involve the numerous actors in society affected by the study and its outcome. Included in this list were women and men using and not using family planning services; service providers at clinics; shopkeepers and community-based distributors; policy-makers; donors to family planning programmes; researchers and NGO staff.

Government and NGO clinic staffs and private service providers were a part of the study's sampling. Similarly, policy-makers in government and NGOs were involved as key informants in the policy review.

For WHAF's appraisal, principal investigators were recruited from the various countries where the study was to be conducted. Those undertaking the study received training in their own language. The questionnaires used were also developed in the local vernacular. This contributed to the easy facilitation of training, data collection, tabulation and a feeling of ownership. Such actions lead to ways to maximize the use of the study's final results.

Research work is notorious for being detached and divorced from the general public. Reports collect dust on the shelves of research organizations and are rarely shared with those who have a stake in them. Researchers are often accused of using 'subjects' to gain merit in their professional career without giving anything back to the community from which they collected their data.

The proposed appraisal process set out in this manual aims at supplying researchers with ways to overcome such problems while granting the greatest exposure and impact to the survey's results. The following ideas can help researchers plan ways to use their end report.

Involve those affected by the research

All of the stakeholders mentioned above – clients and non-clients, service providers, policy-makers, donors, researchers and NGOs – need to be involved in the sharing of the appraisal's results. Define clear recommendations for each of the stakeholders, clarifying what they can specifically contribute to quality of care.

Feedback seminars should be held with the service providers interviewed in the study. Focus group discussions with those who were involved in the appraisal will elicit their opinions on the results. This can be used to validate the findings and to formulate recommendations for action, as a subsequent step in improving the quality of care.

Disseminate the results – publish

A plan for disseminating the findings should be made, including target audiences to be reached, methods by which they can be reached and messages to be stressed.

It is essential that the appraisal results be presented in a report. Summarized articles can also be published. Newspapers, magazines, journals and NGO newsletters can be the vehicles for dissemination. Publication at both the local and national levels ensures reaching a wider audience. Similarly, this can also be done for the regional and international levels. The aim of dissemination is to get as many people as possible aware of the results and to encourage other groups to undertake similar work.

Contact journalists and develop press materials based on the results of the studies, picking out key facts and examples. Also remember to adjust the language used to the target audience.

What about those people who cannot read or do not have access to written materials? There is no reason to exclude this vital segment of society from the dissemination process. In fact, in all probability, they will be most affected by the quality of care and adherence to reproductive rights carried out in their country. Oral presentations, role-plays, theatre and seminars can be used to reach this group.

Hold seminars

Seminars at the local, district and national level can be held to spread the appraisal's results. Approaches will have to differ depending on the audience. More oral presentations, maybe even short skits, depicting some of the most important findings can be presented to less literate audiences. More 'typical' seminars can be held for literate audiences. Facilitation to elicit active feedback from participants is essential.

Use mass communication

The radio is extensively used by people in many countries. Using this means of communication, in addition to television, can hugely expand the number of people informed of the assessment's results. If expertise and funds are available, videos can be developed which carry the message of the appraisal.

Provide information for advocacy groups

The entire appraisal report or a summary of its main findings can be used as a tool for lobbying and advocating for improvement in the quality of reproductive health services. Women's groups active in this field are always searching for material that can be used and quoted to pressure politicians, bureaucrats and others into giving more attention and resources to this issue. Researchers should contact not only relevant women's groups, but also NGOs involved in policy change for better health and community services. The report could add credibility to their argument that much is left to be done in this area.

Train other researchers

The report itself can also be used as a training tool for those who wish to take up similar assessments or studies. The eight-country appraisal coordinated by WHAF was undertaken by a group of women comprising not only researchers, but also programme implementors, policy-makers, doctors and others. This group's background gave the study a woman's health perspective with the added value of professional credibility to ensure its greatest possible impact. This must be an implicit part of the training undertaken with the assistance of the report.

Use other fora

Present the report at other seminars and workshops (not dedicated to the report) at the local, national, regional and international levels. Even when it is not used in its entirety, it can be used partially or quoted to convey the report's message. The report points to the strengths and deficiencies on the provision of family planning services and the adherence to reproductive rights within a selected area. It does not necessarily have to be used to criticize government services. Instead, it can point to the need for improved facilities with the ultimate goal of making reproductive choices and their implementation possible by men and women around the world.

Look for funding

The first thought that comes to mind when discussing utilizing the findings of the appraisal is the need for resources. This should not pose an insurmountable problem. Much can be done within the existing budgets of NGOs and other institutions since research, advocacy and community participation are already a part of their work. Many institutions will lend their facilities for seminars and workshops. Participants can be requested to pay a contribution to defray some of the costs involved. Many community workers are already trained in focus group discussions. They can undertake dissemination of the report through this means as a part of their regular work. Women at the community level may take part in a functional literacy programme, credit scheme or loan plan. These can all be used as vehicles for sharing the report.

Government departments and other institutions holding workshops and seminars could be encouraged to invite a speaker who would present the appraisal results. Organizations undertaking skills-training in order to carry out a similar assessment could include the cost of the manual in their training budget.

The point is to be innovative in finding ways to disseminate the report on a continuing basis. Remember, if there is a will, there's a way!

Summaries of national follow-up activities

The following sections contain highlights from the national follow-up plans already under way by the research teams taking part in WHAF's collaborative study. These examples are intended to give an idea of the kinds of dissemination/recommendation outputs that can take place as part of such an appraisal project. However, these examples are only a selected summary.

Bangladesh The Bangladesh Women's Health Coalition will hold a series of seminars on themes brought out in the research. People attending these events will include women's health advocates, other national development NGOs, government officials and members of the press. More informal workshops will take place with local women's health organizations to discuss more deeply the findings of the research and to look for improvments in the way in which women receive reproductive health services in the country. The research results will also be used internally by the Coalition's staff to improve their research methodology and help to train new research assistants for future projects.

Finland The research team in Finland plans to write some journal and newsletter articles about their research findings. In addition, some of the results have already been incorporated into lessons given to public health nurses in the country. A meeting will also be arranged bringing together providers who took part in the field work. The project's findings of the type of material that is available to clients, with a special emphasis on adolescents, at family planning centres has sparked a new project to analyse further the type of material used in health centres. This project's findings will be summarized and published. Many ideas brought out by the project's work coincide with elements already brought into Finland's national project *Family Planning to the Year 2000*.

Kenya In Kenya, the Ministry of Health has offered to co-fund dissemination workshops planned for each of the districts in which the field work took place. These will be organized by the head researcher in cooperation with the Ministry's district medical officers. They will offer an opportunity for providers to meet with the research team members, discuss the findings and look for ways to improve the quality of services and information given to clients. Before these workshops take place, the national report will be circulated to all of the institutions which took part in the study.

The Netherlands The Women's Health Action Foundation will hold a dialogue to present the national research to private practitioners and the practitioners at the NGO, the Rutgers Foundation, which took part in the research project. A workshop on the quality of care of reproductive and sexual health offered in the Netherlands will be held in close collaboration with the members of the NGO working group 'Platform Women and Health Beijing '95'. An important challenge will be to create strategies to ensure NGO participation in policy advice and decision-making in this field.

Nigeria A joint workshop sponsored by the university directing the research project will be held to discuss the findings of the appraisal. It will place the results of the study within the context of Nigerian family planning policy now in practice. Recommendations made during the workshop will be brought to policy-makers to improve the reproductive health services offered to women.

Notes

1. To read the eight-country appraisals, see this manual's companion book Hardon, A. P. et al. (eds) (1997) *Reproductive Rights in Practice: A Feminist Report on the Quality of Care* (London: Zed Books).

Appendix 1

Adjusting the list of indicators to local realities based on the results of the exploratory phase

The study of documents and key informant interviews conducted in the policy review should do the following.

- Clarify which methods are available in the country (can be used to adjust indicator A1).
- Specify the restrictions that are supposed to be employed by family planning agencies (indicator A3).
- If the institutions providing family planning services have guidelines on counselling, use these to adjust indicators A4 and B1 on the balanced provision of information during consultations with new clients who want to space births. The same should be done with indicator B2 ('adequacy of information on the pill' given to new pill-users) to assess if these guidelines are followed.
- Specify the types of information that are available to clients in the various family planning programmes. Use this information to adjust indicators B3 and B4 to include items that refer to specific types of information, such as package inserts, leaflets on technical aspects of specific methods, general leaflets on the advantages of family planning, and so on.
- Specify which training programmes are available to providers. This information can be used to add elements to indicator D2.
- Indicate if it is the programme's policy to use incentives and disincentives (indicators C1–4).

- Clarify which methods are most commonly used in the country. This information should be used to review indicators D4 and D5 (adequacy of consultation with new pill-users; screening of new IUD-users). If the pill and/or the IUD are *not* the most commonly used methods, then it is advisable to formulate similar indicators for the methods that *are* used most commonly. For example, if the IUD is hardly used, and injectables are very common (as is the case in Thailand), an indicator on the adequacy of consultations with new injectable-users could replace the one on screening of new IUD-users (D5). The medical procedures to be followed in consultations with new pill-users and new IUD-users should be specified to refine the indicators D4 and D5.
- Specify advice to be given to breastfeeding women (indicator D6).
- Add items to the indicator on the appropriate constellation of services (D7). This specification depends on the extent to which the various components of reproductive health are integrated into the service delivery points in the country. Key items can be used to assess the extent to which such integration is in place.

The focus group discussions should clarify what people see as elements of quality of care and what aspects of the services they dislike. The results of these group discussions should allow for adjustments to the indicators that measure the interpersonal aspects of the care provided and the adequacy of the health-care infrastructure. For example:

- indicator A4 on the quality of provider–client interactions
- indicators B1 and B2 on the adequacy of information (items could be added, inquiring if, for example, providers are referring to specific cultural notions about efficacy and safety of contraceptives that are prevalent, and if providers refer to indigenous means of fertility regulation in their counselling efforts)
- indicator D1 on the adequacy of facilities (items can be added such as the presence of a clean toilet, if users consider this to be important; items that are not considered important can be deleted)
- indicator D7 on the appropriate constellation of services.

Appendix 2
Checklists

Checklist 1

Observation and interviews at community-based distribution centres

Introduction

This checklist includes questions for interviews with community-based distributors (Part 1) and for observation of client–provider consultations (Part 2A and 2B).

Each group of questions corresponds to the core quality of care indicators (A, B, C, D) as discussed in Chapter 4.

The checklist can be adapted to make questionnaires and observation lists appropriate to different localities.

Part 1 Interview with community-based distributor (CBD)

Instructions to interviewer: When interviewing CBDs it should be made clear that you are seeking their assistance in finding ways of improving the functioning and quality of the services offered by CBDs in general, and that you are not *evaluating that particular CBD.*

Greeting

My name is __________ and I work for ___________. We are carrying out a survey of clinics and CBDs which provide family planning services. We are interested in learning of your experiences to date in providing family planning services, and would appreciate your input as to how these services could be improved. Would you mind if I ask you a few questions?

A The need for a free and informed choice of contraceptive methods

A1

1. Which contraceptive methods are available?
   Do not read list of methods but probe by asking: Any other methods?
   Record below which methods the CBD provides and, if yes, check if the contraceptives are in stock.

Type of contraceptive	In stock?
A. Combined pills (specify brands)	No Yes
1.	No Yes
2.	No Yes
3.	No Yes
B. Progestin-only pills (specify brands)	No Yes
1.	No Yes
2.	No Yes
3.	No Yes
C. Condoms	No Yes
D. Diaphragms	No Yes
E. Spermicides	No Yes
F. Injectables	
1. Progestin-only	No Yes
2. Combined	No Yes
G. Emergency contraception (specify method)	No Yes
H. Menstrual regulation	No Yes
I. Abortion	No Yes
J. Lactational amenorrhoea method (LAM)	No Yes
K. Other (specify)	No Yes

A2a

2. What advice would you give to a female client who wishes to *space* births?
Do not read list of methods but prompt by asking: Any other methods?

Methods recommended to space births	**Mentioned by respondent (fill in yes or no)**
1. Pill (unspecified)	
2. Combined pill	
3. Progestin-only pill	
4. Condom	
5. Spermicides	
6. Diaphragm	
7. Injectables (unspecified)	
8. Injectables – combined	
9. Injectables – progestin-only	
10. Emergency contraception (specify method)	
11. Menstrual regulation	
12. Abortion	
13. Lactational amenorrhoea method (LAM)	
14. Other methods recommended (specify)	
15. Depends on condition of the client or how suitable method is for client	
16. Depends on what client wants	
Other responses	
17. Refer her to the nearest SDP	
18. Do not recommend any particular method	
19. Don't know	
20. No information given	

A2b

3. What advice would you *never* give to a female client who wishes to space births?
Do not read list of methods but prompt by asking: Any other methods?

Methods never recommended	**Mentioned by respondent (fill in yes or no)**
1. Pill (unspecified)	
2. Combined pill	
3. Progestin-only-pill	
4. Condom	
5. Spermicides	
6. Diaphragm	
7. Injectables (unspecified)	
8. Injectables – combined	
9. Injectables – progestin-only	
10. Emergency contraception (specify method)	
11. Menstrual regulation	
12. Abortion	
13. Lactational amenorrhoea method (LAM)	
14. Other (specify)	
15. Depends on condition of client or how suitable method is for client	
16. Depends on what client wants	
Other responses	
17. Refer her to the nearest SDP	
18. Do not recommend any particular method	
19. Don't know	
20. No information given	

A3a

4. Are there any restrictions other than medical when providing clients with the *contraceptive pill*, i.e. the age of client, number of living children, marital status, consent of spouse, or other restrictions? Describe the restrictions and the reasons for applying them.

Restrictions in provision of the contraceptive pill	**Tick if applicable**	**Describe the *nature* of the restriction and *how* the restriction is verified**	**Specify why the restriction is applied**
1. Age			
2. Number of living children			
3. Marital status			
4. Spousal consent			
5. Other restrictions (specify)			

B Informed choice of methods through the provision of appropriate information

B3

5. Are written IEC (information, education and communication) materials available for clients?
If yes, ask if you may see the IEC materials, and describe them.

0 = no
1 = yes

Description:

C Avoidance of incentives and disincentives that violate reproductive rights

C1

6. Do you, as a CBD, receive benefits/remuneration related to the number of 'acceptors' you have or the number of 'new acceptors' you recruit?

   0 = no
   1 = yes

7. If yes, what kind?
   Description:

C2

8. Are you, as a CBD, sanctioned if certain acceptance targets are not met?

   0 = no
   1 = yes

9. If yes, how?
   Description:

C3

10. Do users/acceptors receive incentives in cash or in kind for accepting contraceptives?

    0 = no
    1 = yes

11. If yes, what kind?
    Description:

12. Are there any sanctions against clients who refuse to use contraceptive methods?

0 = no
1 = yes

13. If yes, what kind?
Description:

D A health-care infrastructure that enables safe fertility regulation

D2

14. Did you receive training in family planning during your vocational training?

0 = no
1 = yes

15. Did you ever receive any on-the-job training in family planning?

0 = no
1 = yes

16. Have you received any (additional) training in family planning in the past three years?

0 = no
1 = yes

17. Did you receive training on contraindications for contraceptive use?

0 = no
1 = yes

18. Did you receive training on how to counsel clients?

0 = no
1 = yes

D6

19. What would you advise a woman who is breastfeeding her six-week-old baby and who has yet to resume menstruating to do about family planning?
Do not prompt, check all that apply. At the end ask: Is there anything else?

Advised method	Tick if mentioned
Appropriate	
1. No method, contraception unnecessary (LAM)	
2. IUD	
3. Progestin-only method	
4. Barrier method	
Inappropriate	
5. Combined hormonal method	
6. Other (specify)	

D7

20. Do you promote condoms to prevent STDs (sexually transmitted diseases) and HIV?

0 = no
1 = yes

21. Do you provide information, education and/or counselling (IEC) on STDs and HIV/AIDS?

0 = no
1 = yes

22. Do you provide information, education and/or counselling on infertility?

0 = no
1 = yes

Part 2A Observation of provider (CBD)/client contact

Below are two observation lists, one for provider/new client contact and one for provider/resupply client contact. Use the appropriate observation list for the provider/client contact you observe.

For each of the questions listed below, enter the code that represents your observation of what happened during the interaction.

New client

23. Sex of the provider

0 = male
1 = female

24. Sex of the client

0 = male
1 = female

A. The need for a free and informed choice of contraceptive methods

A4a

25. Did the provider greet the client in a respectful and/or friendly manner?

0 = no
1 = yes

26. Did the provider inquire about the reproductive plans and/or the contraceptive intentions of the client?

0 = no
1 = yes

27. Did the provider discuss methods other than the one accepted by the client?

0 = no
1 = yes

28. Did the provider encourage the client to decide her/himself on the contraceptive to use?

0 = no
1 = yes

29. Did the provider ask the client whether s/he wanted to ask a question?

0 = no
1 = yes

30. Did the provider listen attentively to the client?

0 = no
1 = yes

B Informed choice of methods through the provision of appropriate information

B1

31. Check *which* of the following methods were discussed. Also, check *which aspects* of the following methods were discussed with the client; and if samples of one or more methods were shown.

Method	**Tick if mentioned**
Contraceptive pill	
1. How to use	
2. Effectiveness	
3. Side effects	
4. No protection against STDs and HIV/AIDS	
5. That the pill can cause changes in menstrual cycle	
IUD	
1. Effectiveness	
2. How administered	
3. Side effects	
4. Risks related to STDs	
5. Can cause heavy bleeding during menstruation	

Method	Tick if mentioned
Injectables	
1. Effectiveness	
2. How administered	
3. Side effects	
4. Can cause changes in menstrual cycle	
Condom	
1. How to use	
2. Effectiveness	
3. Prevention of STDs	

B2

32. Check if any of the following items were discussed when the provider talked about the contraceptive pill. *Only conduct this observation with new pill-user consultations.*

Contraceptive pill. Topics discussed	Tick if mentioned
1. How it works	
2. How to use it	
3. What to do if a pill is missed	
4. Side effects	
5. Possible changes in menstrual cycle	
6. Risks related to smoking	
7. What to do if side effects occur	
8. No protection against HIV/AIDS	
9. Need to use condoms as well if client is at risk for HIV/AIDS	
10. When and where to get resupply	
11. Sample of pills shown	

33. Did provider give any written materials to client?

0 = no
1 = yes

D Health-care infrastructure that enables safe fertility regulation

D1

34. Check which of the following items are present or available at the SDP. *If you are not able to see this yourself during the observation, please ask the selected provider to show you.*

Item	Tick if present
1. CBD record book	
2. CBD handbook/manual	
3. Written material for clients	
4. Addresses of referral clinics	
5. Checklist of contraindications for the pill	

D3

35. Was the client's medical history taken?

0 = no
1 = yes

36. Was pregnancy excluded?

0 = no
1 = yes

37. If yes, how?

38. Was the client informed about when to return for a follow-up visit?

0 = no
1 = yes

D4

39. *The following observation* only *with new clients who chose to use the contraceptive pill.*

- Was the new contraceptive pill-user screened for contraindications?

- Check which of the following items was discussed or verified with the client.

	Tick if discussed/verified
1. Smoking	
2. Blood pressure taken	
3. Use of medicines	
4. Breastfeeding	
5. Diarrhoea and/or vomiting	

Resupply client

A4b

40. Did provider greet client in a respectful and/or friendly manner?

0 = no
1 = yes

41. Did the provider inquire about the experiences of the client with the method used?

0 = no
1 = yes

42. Did the provider listen attentively?

0 = no
1 = yes

Part 2B Researcher's observation

To be completed after the interaction.

Please describe below your overall impressions of the interaction, with specific reference to the strengths and weaknesses of the CBD. Use your own judgement and try to put yourself in the position of the client. In particular, please comment on whether or not the terms that the CBD used with the client were understood by the client. Did the provider react according to the client's wishes if the client had any problems or wanted to change methods? Include any suggestions you may have for improving the quality of the interaction.

Checklist 2

Observation of service delivery points (SDPs) and interview schedule for staff providing family planning at SDPs

Introduction

This checklist includes questions for interviews with staff of a service delivery point for family planning services (Part 1) and for observation of client–provider consultations (Part 2A and B).

Each group of questions corresponds to the core quality of care indicators (A, B, C, D) as discussed in Chapter 4.

The checklist can be adapted to make questionnaires and observation lists appropriate to different localities.

Part 1 Interview with key informant at service delivery point (SDP)

This checklist is to be used for interview with key informant at the SDP.

Description of centre.

1. Type of SDP (*circle one*)
   a. private clinic
   b. rural health centre (governmental)
   c. urban clinic in poor area (governmental)
   d. urban clinic in residential area (governmental)
   e. mission clinic
   f. non-government clinic (*specify*) ______________
   g. other ________________________

2. What referral mechanisms exist? Where are clients referred to and for which services?

____

____

____

3. Approximate number of women served in population (in terms of reproductive-age women). *Use local definition of fertile age: for example 15–49 or 15–45.*

____

4. How many days per week are family planning services available, and how many hours per day?

____

____

5. Does a medical doctor provide family planning services at this SDP?

   0 = no
   1 = yes

6. If yes, is this doctor male or female?

   0 = male
   1 = female

7. How many paramedical staff (i.e. nurses, midwives, etc.) provide family planning services at this SDP?

____

____

8. Does this SDP have any staff vacancies?

   0 = no
   1 = yes

9. How far is the nearest referral source (hospital, etc.) for emergency aid?

____

10. Designation of staff member who is interviewed:
Circle one

1. doctor
2. nurse/midwife
3. paramedical staff person
   (*specify*) ______________________________
4. other ______________________________

11. What is the male/female ratio of clients visiting the clinic? Do men ever visit? If never, or rarely, why is this so?

    ____

    ____

    ____

12. What is the profile of the clients visiting?
    1. proportion of new clients and proportion of resupply clients
    2. marital status
    3. age-distribution
    4. number of children

    ____

    ____

    ____

A The need for a free and informed choice of contraceptive methods

A1

13. Which contraceptive methods are available? *Do not read list of methods but prompt by asking:* Any other methods? *Record below which methods the SDP provides and, if yes, check if the contraceptives are* in stock.

Type of contraceptive	In stock?
A. Combined pills (specify brands)	
1.	No Yes
2.	No Yes
3.	No Yes
B. Progestin-only pills (specify brands)	
1.	No Yes
2.	No Yes
3.	No Yes

Type of contraceptive	In stock?
C. Condoms	No Yes
D. Diaphragms	No Yes
E. Spermicides	No Yes
F. IUD (specify)	No Yes
1. Copper T 380A	No Yes
2. Lippes®	No Yes
3. Multiload 250®	No Yes
4. Multiload 375®	No Yes
5. Other ____________________	No Yes
G. Injectables	
1. Progestin-only	No Yes
2. Combined	No Yes
H. Female sterilization	
1. Minilap, local anaesthetic	No Yes
2. Minilap, general anaesthetic	No Yes
3. Laparotomy	No Yes
I. Vasectomy	No Yes
J. Norplant®	No Yes
K. 'Natural' family planning	No Yes
L. Emergency contraception (specify method)	No Yes
M. Menstrual regulation	No Yes
N. Abortion	No Yes
O. Lactational amenorrohea method (LAM)	No Yes
K. Other (specify)	No Yes

A2a

14. What advice would you give to a female client who wishes to *space* births? *Do not read list of methods but prompt by asking:* Any other methods?

Methods recommended	Mentioned by respondent (fill in yes or no)
1. Pill (unspecified)	
2. Combined pill	
3. Progestin-only pill	
4. Condom	

Methods recommended	**Mentioned by respondent (fill in yes or no)**
5. Spermicides	
6. Diaphragm	
7. Injectables (unspecified)	
8. Injectables – progestin only	
9. Injectables – combined	
10. IUD	
11. Female sterilization (tubal ligation)	
12. Male sterilization (vasectomy)	
13. Norplant®	
14. Natural family planning	
15. Emergency contraception (specify method)	
16. Menstrual regulation	
17. Abortion	
18. Lactational amenorrhoea method (LAM)	
19. Other (specify)	
20. Depends on condition of the client or how suitable method is for client	
21. Depends on what client wants	
Other responses	
22. Refer her to the nearest SDP	
23. Do not recommend any particular method: support family planning	
24. Do not recommend any method: against family planning	
25. Don't know	
26. No information given	

A2b

15. What advice would you *never* give to a female client who wishes to space births?
Do not read list of methods but prompt by asking: Any other methods?

Methods recommended	Mentioned by respondent (fill in yes or no)
1. Pill (unspecified)	
2. Combined pill	
3. Progestin-only pill	
4. Condom	
5. Spermicides	
6. Diaphragm	
7. Injectables (unspecified)	
8. Injectables – progestin only	
9. Injectables – combined	
10. IUD	
11. Female sterilization (tubal ligation)	
12. Male sterilization (vasectomy)	
13. Norplant®	
14. Natural family planning	
15. Emergency contraception (specify method)	
16. Menstrual regulation	
17. Abortion	
18. Lactational amenorrhoea method (LAM)	
19. Other (specify)	
20. Depends on condition of the client or how suitable method is for client	
21. Depends on what client wants	
Other responses	
22. Refer her to the nearest SDP	
23. Do not recommend any particular method: support family planning	
24. Do not recommend any method: against family planning	
25. Don't know	
26. No information given	

A3a

16. Are there any restrictions related to when providing clients with the *contraceptive pill*, the age of client, number of living children,

marital status, consent of spouse, or other restrictions? Describe the restrictions and the reasons for applying them.

Restrictions in provision of contraceptive pill	**Tick if applicable**	**Describe the *nature* of the restriction and *how* the restriction is verified**	**Specify why the restriction is applied**
1. Age			
2. Number of living children			
3. Marital status			
4. Spousal consent			
5. Other restrictions (specify)			

A3b

17. Are there any such restrictions applied to clients who wish to be *sterilized*? Describe the restrictions and the reasons for applying them.

Restrictions in provision of sterilization	**Tick if applicable**	**Describe the *nature* of the restriction and *how* the restriction is verified**	**Specify why the restriction is applied**
1. Age a. female b. male			
2. Number of children a. female b. male			

3. Marital status a. female b. male			
4. Spousal consent a. female b. male			
5. Other restrictions (specify) a. female b. male			

A3c

18. Are there any such restrictions applied to clients who wish to use the IUD? Describe the restrictions and the reasons for applying them. *Ask what the exact age is above or under which access to the IUD is restricted and why, and describe qualitatively what the age restrictions are. Ask how the restrictions are verified and in what manner. For example, how is marital status verified and in what manner is spousal consent obtained (written, oral). Do the same for the other restrictions.*

Restrictions in provision of UID	**Tick if applicable**	**Describe the *nature* of the restriction and *how* the restriction is verified**	**Specify why the restriction is applied**
1. Age			
2. Number of living children			
3. Marital status			
4. Spousal consent			
5. Other restrictions (specify)			

B Informed choice of methods through the provision of appropriate information

B3

19. Are written IEC (information, education and communication) materials available for clients? *If yes, ask if you may see the IEC materials, and describe them.*

o = no
1 = yes

Description:

C Avoidance of incentives and disincentives that violate reproductive rights

C1

20. Do you, as a provider, receive benefits/remuneration related to the number of 'acceptors' you have or the number of 'new acceptors' you recruit?

o = no
1 = yes

21. If yes, what kind?
Description:

C2

22. Are you, as a provider, sanctioned if certain acceptance targets are not met?

o = no
1 = yes

23. If yes, how so?
Description:

C3

24. Do users/acceptors receive incentives in cash or kind for accepting contraceptives?

0 = no
1 = yes

25. If yes, what kind?
Description:

26. Are there any sanctions against clients who refuse to use contraceptive methods in your clinic?

0 = no
1 = yes

27. If yes, what kind?
Description:

D A health-care infrastructure that enables safe fertility-regulation methods

D1

28. Check if the following items are present or available at the SDP. Ask the respondent if you can see each item. *Check which of the following items are present or available at the SDP.*

Item	Tick if present/ available
1. Space for changing/undressing where privacy is guaranteed	
2. Separate room/examination area where privacy is guaranteed	
3. Clean examination area	
4. Water available	
5. Blood-pressure cuff	
6. Vaginal speculum	
7. Examination table	
8. Equipment for sterilization/boiling of medical instruments	

Item	Tick if present/ available
9. Covered bin for needles and syringes	
10. Sterile gloves	
11. Disinfectant	
12. Inventory of supplies	
13. Records of clients	
14. Written guidelines for family planning methods	
15. Written information materials for clients	
16. Pre-packaged, sterile IUDs	
18. Addresses of available referral centres	

D2

29. Did you receive training in family planning in the curriculum of your professional training?

    0 = no
    1 = yes

30. Did you ever receive any on-the-job training in family planning?

    0 = no
    1 = yes

31. Have you received any (additional) training in family planning in the past three years?

    0 = no
    1 = yes

32. Did you receive training on contraindications for contraceptive use?

    0 = no
    1 = yes

33. Did you receive training on how to counsel clients?

    0 = no
    1 = yes

D6

34. What would you advise a woman who is breastfeeding her six-week-old baby and who has yet to resume menstruating to do about family planning? *Do not prompt, check all that apply. At the end ask:* Is there anything else?

Advised method	**Tick if mentioned**
Appropriate	
1. No method, contraception unnecessary (LAM)	
2. IUD	
3. Progestin-only pill	
4. Barrier method	
Inappropriate	
5. Combined hormonal method	
6. Other (specify)	

D7

35. Does this SDP promote condoms to prevent STDs (sexually transmitted diseases) and HIV?

0 = no
1 = yes

36. Does this SDP provide information, education and/or counselling (IEC) on STDs and HIV/AIDS?

0 = no
1 = yes

37. Can laboratory tests for STDs be done at this SDP?

0 = no
1 = yes

38. Can you refer clients for such tests?

0 = no
1 = yes

39. Are STDs treated at this SDP?

0 = no
1 = yes

40. Do you provide counselling on infertility?

0 = no
1 = yes

41. Does this SDP provide (simple) diagnostic tests for infertility?

0 = no
1 = yes

42. Does this SDP provide abortion services?

0 = no
1 = yes

43. Does this SDP provide emergency contraception?

0 = no
1 = yes

44. Is this SDP involved in services aimed at screening for reproductive cancers?

0 = no
1 = yes

45. Does this SDP conduct counselling on sexuality?

0 = no
1 = yes

46. The Ministry of Health would like to make sure that the family planning services are meeting people's needs and that the services provided are of the highest quality possible. Do you have any suggestions for ways in which the FP services could be improved?

Part 2A Observation of provider (SDP)/ client contact

Below are two observation lists, one for provider/new client contact and one for provider/resupply client contact. Use the appropriate observation list for the provider/client contact you observe.

For each of the questions listed below, enter the code that represents your observation of what happened during the interaction.

New client

47. Sex of the provider

o = male
1 = female

48. Sex of the client

o = male
1 = female

A The need for a free and informed choice of contraceptive methods

A4a

49. Did the provider greet the client in a respectful and/or friendly manner?

o = no
1 = yes

50. Did the provider inquire about the reproductive plans and/or the contraceptive intentions of the client?

o = no
1 = yes

51. Did the provider discuss methods other than the one accepted by the client?

o = no
1 = yes

52. Did the provider encourage the client to decide her/himself on the contraceptive to use?

o = no
1 = yes

53. Did the provider ask the client whether s/he wanted to ask a question?

0 = no
1 = yes

54. Did the provider listen attentively to the client?

0 = no
1 = yes

B Informed choice of methods through the provision of appropriate information

B1

55. Check *which* of the following methods were discussed. Also, check *which aspects* of the following methods were discussed with the client.

Method	**Tick if mentioned**
Contraceptive pill	
1. How to use	
2. How effective	
3. Side effects	
4. No protection against STDs and HIV/AIDS	
5. Can cause changes in menstrual cycle	
IUD	
1. Effectiveness	
2. How administered	
3. Side effects	
4. Risks related to STDs	
5. Can cause heavy bleeding during menstruation	
Injectables	
1. Effectiveness	
2. How administered	
3. Side effects	
4. Can cause changes in menstrual cycle	
Condom	
1. How to use	
2. Effectiveness	
3. Prevention of STDs	

56. Check whether samples of the following methods are shown to the client.

Samples	Tick if shown
1. Contraceptive pill	
2. IUD	
3. Injectable	
4. Condom	

B2

57. Check if any of the following items were discussed when the provider talked about the contraceptive pill. *Only conduct this observation with new pill-user consultations.*

Contraceptive pill. Topics discussed	Tick if mentioned
1. How it works	
2. How to use it	
3. What to do if a pill is missed	
4. Side effects	
5. Possible changes in menstrual cycle	
6. Risks related to smoking	
7. What to do if side effects occur	
8. No protection against HIV/AIDS	
9. Need to use condoms as well if client is at risk for HIV/AIDS	
10. When and where to get resupply	
11. Sample of pills shown	

D Health-care infrastructure that enables safe fertility regulation

D3

58. Was the client's medical history taken?

0 = no
1 = yes

59. Was pregnancy excluded?

0 = no
1 = yes

60. If yes, how?

____

61. Was the client informed about when to return for a follow-up visit?

0 = no
1 = yes

D4

62. *The following question* only *for clients who chose to use the contraceptive pill:*

- Was the new contraceptive pill-user screened for contraindications?
- Check which of the following items was discussed or verified with the client.

	Tick if discussed/verified
1. Smoking	
2. Blood pressure taken	
3. Use of medicines	
4. Breastfeeding	
5. Diarrhoea and/or vomiting	

D5

63. *The following question* only *for clients who chose to use an IUD.*

- Was the new IUD-user screened for reproductive tract infections?

0 = no
1 = yes

- Check which of the following procedures was performed or verified by the provider.

	Tick if performed/ verified
1. Performs pelvic examination	
2. Asks client about vaginal discharge	
3. Asks whether client has multiple sex partners	
4. Asks whether partner is likely to have multiple sex partners	
5. Advises client to have laboratory test done / has test done	

Resupply client

A4b

64. Did provider greet client in a respectful and/or friendly manner?

0 = no
1 = yes

65. Did the provider inquire about the experiences of the client with the method used?

0 = no
1 = yes

66. Did the provider listen attentively?

0 = no
1 = yes

Part 2B Researcher's observations

To be completed after the interaction.

Please describe below your overall impressions of the interaction, with specific reference to the strengths and weaknesses of the provider. Use your own judgement and try to put yourself in the position of the client. In particular, please comment on whether or not the terms that the provider used with the client were understood by the client. Did the provider react according to the client's wishes if the client had any problems or wanted to change methods?

Also consider gender issues. What was the sex of the provider and the client? Does the sex of the provider affect the quality of the counselling? Include any suggestions you may have for improving the quality of the interaction.

Checklist 3

Exit questionnaire for family planning clients attending the service delivery point

Introduction

This checklist includes questions for exit interviews with new clients at a service delivery point (SDP) for family planning services. Each group of questions corresponds to the core quality of care indicators (A, B, C, D) as discussed in Chapter 4. The checklist can be adapted to make questionnaires appropriate to different localities.

Exit interview with family planning clients

Instructions to the interviewer: When a family planning client has finished her/his consultation with the SDP staff, ask her/him if s/he is willing to answer a few questions about the service s/he has received. It is essential that you gain her/his informed consent before beginning the interview, so the following introduction should be given.

(NB: This interview should not be done by the same person who observed the consultation of the client with the provider.)

Greeting

Hello. We would be interested in finding out your feelings about the service you have received. I would like to ask you a few questions about the meeting you have just had with the clinic staff and would be very grateful if you could spend a little time talking with me.

I will not write down your name. Everything you tell me will be kept strictly confidential. Your participation is voluntary and you are not obliged to answer any questions you do not want to.

Do I have your permission to continue?

A The need for a free and informed choice of contraceptive methods

A5

1. Is this your first visit to the family planning service, or have you been here before? Are you coming for resupply?

   0 = been before (*Stop interview and find another client.*)
   1 = first visit
   2 = resupply client

2. Did you come here to request the supply of a specific contraceptive method?

   0 = no
   1 = yes

3. If yes, did you receive this specific method?

   0 = no
   1 = yes

4. If no, why not? Specify:

   ____

5. *Next question only for new contraceptive pill-users.*
   Did the provider/clinic staff give you information about the contraceptive pill?
   Read each of the questions and tick appropriate box.
   Did s/he …

Question	No	Yes	Don't know
1. explain clearly how the pill works?			
2. explain to you how to use the pill?			
3. explain what to do if a pill is forgotten?			
4. describe possible side effects?			

Question	No	Yes	Don't know
5. explain possible changes in your menstrual cycle?			
6. explain the risks related to smoking?			
7. tell you what to do if you had side effects?			
8. explain that the pill does not protect against HIV transmission?			
9. explain that you need to use condoms in combination with the pill as well if you are at risk?			
10. tell you where to get a resupply of pills?			
11. show you a sample of the pills?			

6. Did you understand what the provider explained to you about the use of the contraceptive pill?

   0 = no
   1 = yes
   9 = partially

B Informed choice of methods through the provision of appropriate information

B4

7. Did you receive written information?

   0 = no *(go to question 11)*
   1 = yes

8. If yes, may I see it?

   0 = no
   1 = yes

9. Is it written in the language that you speak?

   0 = no
   1 = yes

10. Is this written information clear to you?

   0 = no
   1 = yes
   9 = partially

11. Do you feel that the provider/clinic staff listened to you during the consultation?

 0 = no
 1 = yes

12. Do you find that you received the information you wanted during today's consultation?

 0 = no
 1 = yes

C Avoidance of incentives and disincentives that violate reproductive rights

C3

13. Did you receive any incentive in cash or kind for accepting contraceptives?

 0 = no
 1 = yes

14. If yes, what kind?

____

____

____

C4

15. What would happen if you decided not to use contraceptives? Would you be penalized with regard to access to health services?

 0 = no
 1 = yes

16. If yes, how?

____

____

____

D A health-care infrastructure that enables safe fertility regulation

D4

17. *The following question* only *for new clients who chose to use the contraceptive pill.*

- Was the new contraceptive pill-user screened for contraindications?
- Check which of the following items was discussed or verified with the client.

	Tick if discussed/verified
1. Smoking	
2. Blood pressure taken	
3. Use of medicines	
4. Breastfeeding	
5. Diarrhoea and / or vomiting	

D5

18. *The following question only for new clients who chose to use an IUD.*

- Was the new IUD-user screened for reproductive tract infections?
- Check which of the following procedures was performed or verified by the provider.

	Tick if performed/ verified
1. Performs a pelvic examination	
2. Asks a client about vaginal discharge	
3. Asks whether client has multiple sex partners	
4. Ask whether client's partner is likely to have multiple sex partners?	
5. Advises client to have a laboratory test done/has test done	

To end with, I would like to ask you a few questions about yourself and your family.

19. How old are you?
    Code years mentioned

    8 = don't know
    9 = no answer

20. What is your marital status?

    1 = married/monogamous
    2 = married/polygamous
    3 = cohabitating
    4 = single, never married
    5 = divorced/separated/widowed
    9 = no answer

21. How many living children of your own do you have?
    How many boys:
    How many girls:

22. Sex of exit-client

    0 = male
    1 = female

Thank you very much for taking the time to answer these questions.

Checklist 4

Guidelines and questions for focus group discussions (FGDs)

Introduction

The purpose of the focus group discussion is to obtain information about where users obtain contraceptives in the research area and how users and non-users value the services at each source.

Groups:

1. Adolescents
2. Women/men with no children
3. Women/men with one or two children, intending to space births
4. Women/men with completed families

Guidelines and questions

1. What do you/people do to prevent or delay pregnancy?
   Prompt by asking: What methods or practices are available?
   List all practices, including traditional methods and cultural practices. Draw them or write the names of the method on pieces of paper to serve as visual aids.

2. What are the advantages and disadvantages of each method and/or practice?
   Ask about the cost of the methods and about people's willingness and ability to pay.
   Use the visual aids mentioned above.

3. Who uses the method – men, women, adolescents?
   If relevant, ask why men do not use methods.
   Use the visual aids mentioned above.

4. Does unwanted pregnancy occur? Why does it happen? What do people do when unwanted pregnancy occurs?
   List all practices, including traditional methods and cultural practices. Draw them or write the names of the method on pieces of paper to serve as visual aids.

5. Where do you go to obtain your fertility-regulating methods? List all sources. *Prompt by asking:* Any other sources?

6. In your opinion, what are the advantages and disadvantages of the various sources?
   Ask about what the FGD members view as important in the offered services.

7. Who uses the services - men, women, adolescents?
   Ask about the cost of services.
   Also ask about the constellation of services, which services are offered, which not.
   If relevant, ask why men do not use the services.

C Avoidance of incentives and disincentives that violate reproductive rights

C3

8. Were you promised any incentive in cash or kind to use/accept a contraceptive? If so, did you receive the promised incentive?
   List all kinds of incentives mentioned.

C4

9. What would happen if you decided not to use contraceptives? Would you be penalized, for example, with regard to access to health services?
Prompt by asking: Any other kind of sanctions?
List all kinds of sanctions and/or penalizing measures FGD members mention.

Bibliography

Aitken, I. and Reichenbach, L. (1994) 'Reproductive and Sexual Health Services: Expanding Access and Enhancing Quality', in G. Sen et al. (eds), *Population Policies Reconsidered: Health, Empowerment and Rights*, Harvard Series on Population and International Health (Boston, MA: Harvard University Press).

Alcala, M. (1994) *Action for the 21st Century. Reproductive Health and Rights For All: Summary Report of Recommended Actions of Reproductive Health and Rights in the Cairo ICPD Program of Action* (New York: Family Care International).

Berer, M. (1993) 'Population and Family Planning Policies: Women-Centred Perspective', *Reproductive Health Matters* 1: 4–12.

Bruce, J. (1990) 'Fundamental Elements of the Quality of Care: A Simple Framework', *Studies in Family Planning* 21(2): 61–91.

Corrêa, S. (1994) *Population and Reproductive Rights: Feminist Perspectives from the South*, Development Alternatives with Women for a New Era (DAWN) (London: Zed Books).

Donabedian, A. (1988) 'The Quality of Care: How Can It Be Assessed?', *Journal of the American Medical Association* 260(12): 1743–8.

Evaluation Project (1993) *Indicators of Quality of Care in International Family Planning Programs* (Chapel Hill, SC: University of South Carolina, Carolina Population Center).

Fisher, A. et al. (1992) *Guidelines and Instruments for a Family Planning Situation Analysis Study* (New York: Population Council).

Garcia-Moreno, C. and Claro, A. (1994) 'Challenges from the Women's Health Movement: Women's Rights Versus Population Control', in G. Sen et al. (eds), *Population Policies Reconsidered: Health, Empowerment and Rights*, Harvard Series on Population and International Health (Boston, MA: Harvard University Press).

Green, E. C. (1988) 'A Consumer Intercept Study of Oral Contraceptive Users in the Dominican Republic', *Studies in Family Planning* 19(2): 109–17.

Hardon, A. P. (1992) 'The Needs of Women Versus the Interests of Family Planning Personnel, Policy-makers and Researchers: Conflicting Views on Safety and Acceptability of Contraceptives', *Social Science and Medicine* 35(6): 753–66.

Hardon, A. P. et al. (eds) (1994) *Applied Health Research Manual* (Amsterdam: Spinhuis).

Hardon, A. P. et al. (eds) (1997) *Reproductive Rights in Practice* (London: Zed).

Hart, C. (1991) 'Enterprise and QA', in *The Quality of Family Planning Services in Field Projects: A Workshop Report,* SEATS, Columbia University, 18–20 June.

Hartmann, B. (1987) *Reproductive Rights and Wrongs: The Global Politics of Population Control and Contraceptive Choice* (New York: Harper and Row).

Hartmann, B. and Standing, H. (1985) *Food, Saris and Sterilization: Population Control in Bangladesh* (London: Bangladesh International Action Group).

Helzner, J. F. and Kopp, S. Z. (1991) 'Quality of Care in Family Planning: Perspectives from IPPF/Western Hemisphere Region', Draft report, 1 March.

International Planned Parenthood Federation (IPPF)/IWRAW (1995) Reproductive Rights Wall Chart (London: IPPF Distribution Unit).

Jain, A. K. (ed.) (1992) *Managing Quality of Care in Population Programs*, 18 (West Hartford, CT: Kumarian Press).

Katz, K. et al. (1993) *Quality of Care in Family Planning: A Catalog of Assessment and Improvement Tools* (Durham, NC: Family Health International).

Kaufman, J. and Mensch, B. (1992) *Report on the Meeting on Quality of Care and Clinic Based MIS* (New York: Population Council).

Koenig, M. et al. (1992) 'The Influence of Fieldworker Quality of Care upon Contraceptive Adoption in Rural Bangladesh', Paper presented at the annual meeting of the Population Association of America, Denver, 30 April–2 May.

Lynam, P. et al. (1993) 'Using Self-Assessment to Improve the Quality of Family Planning Clinic Services', *Studies in Family Planning* 24(4): 252–60.

Mensch, B. (1993) 'Quality of Care: A Neglected Dimension', in M. Koblinsky et al. (eds), *The Health of Women: A Global Perspective,* (San Francisco: Westview Press).

Miller, R. A. et al. (1992) 'Situation Analysis Study of Kenya's Family Planning Program', in A. K. Jain (ed.), *Managing Quality of Care in Population Programs.*

Mintzes, B. et al. (eds) (1993) *Norplant: Under Her Skin* (Delft: Women's Health Action Foundation and Eburon).

Population Council (1992) *Nigeria: The Family Planning Situational Analysis Study* (New York: Population Council, Africa Operations Research and Technical Assistance Project).

Rabinovitz, L. M. et al. (1993) 'Client and Service Provider Perspectives on Quality of Care: An Evaluation of COPE in Africa', unpublished report (Washington, DC: Association for Voluntary Surgical Contraception [AVSC]).

Ross, J. A. and Isaacs, S. L. (1988) 'Costs, Payments and Incentives in Family Planning Programs: A Review for Developing Countries', *Studies in Family Planning* 19(5): 270–83.

Simmons, R. (1991) 'Methodologies for Studying Clients' Interactions.', Paper presented at the seminar on Client Relations and Quality of Care (New York: Population Council).

Simmons, R. et al. (1986) 'Client Relations in South Asia: Programmatic and Societal Determinants', *Studies in Family Planning* 17(6): 257–68.

Tomaševski, K. (1994) *Human Rights in Population Policies: A Study for SIDA* (Lund, Sweden: SIDA).

United Nations (1968) *Final Act of the International Conference on Human Rights*, A/Conf.32/41 (New York: UN).

— (1974) *Report of the United Nations World Population Conference*, A/Conf.60/19, (New York: UN).

— (1979) *UN Convention on the Elimination of All Forms of Discrimination Against Women (CEDAW)*, GAOR Supplement No. 21, A/34/46, UN Doc. A/Res/34/180 (New York: UN).

— (1994) ICPD *Program of Action* (UN International Conference on Population and Development; text dated 19 September 1994) (New York: ICPD Secretariat).

United Nations FAO (1988) *Conducting Small Scale Nutrition Studies: A Field Manual by FAO.*

Women's Health Action Foundation/WEMOS (1991) 'Guidelines for the Distribution and Use of Fertility Regulating Methods', in B. Mintzes et al. (eds), *A Question of Control* (Amsterdam: WHAF/WEMOS and Health Action International [HAI-Europe]).

World Health Organization (1988) *Health Systems Research Training Course.*

Index